SUPERVISING PRINCIPALS FOR INSTRUCTIONAL LEADERSHIP

SUPERVISING PRINCIPALS FOR INSTRUCTIONAL LEADERSHIP

A Teaching and Learning Approach

Meredith I. Honig and Lydia R. Rainey

Harvard Education Press
Cambridge, Massachusetts

Second Printing, 2021

Paperback ISBN 978-1-68253-464-9
Library Edition ISBN 978-1-68253-465-6

Library of Congress Cataloging-in-Publication Data

Names: Honig, Meredith I., 1971- author. | Rainey, Lydia, author.
Title: Supervising principals for instructional leadership : a teaching and learning approach / Meredith I. Honig and Lydia R. Rainey.
Description: Cambridge, Massachusetts : Harvard Education Press, [2020] | Includes index. | Summary: "Supervising Principals for Instructional Leadership specifies the conditions that district leaders can implement to help principal supervisors take a teaching and learning approach to their work"— Provided by publisher.
Identifiers: LCCN 2019058971 | ISBN 9781682534649 (paperback) | ISBN 9781682534656 (library binding)
Subjects: LCSH: School principals—United States. | Educational leadership—United States. | Educational change—United States. | School personnel management—United States.
Classification: LCC LB2831.9 .H66 2020 | DDC 371.2/012—dc23
LC record available at https://lccn.loc.gov/2019058971

Published by Harvard Education Press,
an imprint of the Harvard Education Publishing Group

Harvard Education Press
8 Story Street
Cambridge, MA 02138

Cover Design: Wilcox Design
Cover Image: Colors Hunter-Chausseur de Couleurs/Moment via Getty Images

The typefaces in this book are Sabon and Futura.

Contents

Acknowledgments

There was no other place we wanted to be at that moment than observing how a principal supervisor was running a meeting for her group of district principals. For one thing, the meeting was out of state in February, a perfect month to be on the road and away from Seattle's long, dark, and wet winter days. The principal supervisor was also just plain inspiring. We had observed her run these meetings about twice a month for a year, and at this point we knew from our initial data analysis that we were in a master class on principals' instructional leadership.

Still, as the last principals left the room shortly after the meeting concluded, the principal supervisor deeply exhaled, smiled at us, and asked, "How do you think that went?" We asked, "Why are you wondering that?" She replied, "I don't know—I mean, I *do* know. I know it's the right work. But don't you sometimes just want someone to say, 'Hey, here is what it looks like when you do your job well, and you are doing great'? Maybe even throw in a 'You go, girl!'?"

Over the next decade, we often found ourselves in similar conversations—with principal supervisors and other central office leaders. These leaders were confident enough in their ideas to be leading fundamental changes in their central offices, but occasionally struggling with whether or not they were on the right track. They asked for role models, or research, or clear enough feedback, or something else to assure them. Sometimes, those leaders would give in to the struggle and abandon their efforts, falling back on long-standing ways of working in their central offices. Others would find the resources to stay the course. Some principal supervisors generously told us that they found our early journal articles and reports helpful guides for the course. But, they asked, didn't we have something else—anything that brings it all together in one place?

This volume is our attempt at that something else. The findings we share here stem from those original research articles and reports but reach beyond them as we have continued analyzing our original research findings, collecting and analyzing new data, and partnering with districts across the country trying to transform their central offices into engines of true educational equity. Over the years, we have had tremendous opportunities to walk and learn alongside principal supervisors and other central office leaders as they went about that important and challenging work. At this point, we have a consistent set of research-based ideas and advice. When principal supervisors work in ways aligned with that advice, we now predictably see positive results. When principal supervisors continue with traditional forms of principal supervision, we predictably don't.

Our main goal with this volume is to honor the leaders who have been so generous with us—who opened up their practice, shared their thinking, tried and tried again, and also encouraged us to write this book. We also aim to make the lessons we have already learned together even more accessible to other district leaders so they can build on what we know, avoid predictable mistakes, and, ultimately, design even more powerful approaches to central office change to address their persistent and still elusive promise of educational equity. This volume and the work that preceded it would not have been possible without those leaders and their trust in us. Our confidential agreements preclude us from naming them. We hope they see their influence and inspiration in the following pages.

We also acknowledge and deeply appreciate the assistance and support of many others who helped us stay our course. Mike Copland was our first co-Principal Investigator and collaborator on our central office transformation research. He always reminded us that if we truly care about educational equity, supporting systems-focused leaders is some of the most important work we can do.

Over the years, many research assistants have helped us collect and analyze data, conduct literature reviews, and push our thinking. Special thanks to: Emily Donaldson Walsh, Alyson M. Honsa, Juli Lawton, Patricia McNeil, Jenee Myers Twitchell, Morena Newton, and Nitya Venkateswaran.

The Wallace Foundation generously supported our initial research study as well as our subsequent efforts to move our findings into standards, tools, and other resources for the field. We are extremely grateful for their belief in our work and their ongoing national leadership. The W. T. Grant Foundation and the Spencer Foundation helped us deepen our program of research, including our investigations into small school districts and how to support district leaders as they reimagine long-standing institutions like principal supervision. We thank them again and again for their encouragement and partnership.

We may not have written this book any time soon without the repeated nudges from Dr. Rochelle Herring. Her feedback helped us think about this volume in just the right ways.

Harvard Education Press has been the perfect press for book, given the high value they place of putting rigorous scholarship to work for practitioners. Thank you, Caroline Chauncey, for the encouragement and extremely helpful advice and feedback right when we needed it, and to the whole HEP team for the care they took with our project.

We dedicate this book to our professor and colleague, Mike Knapp. The consummate teacher and mentor, when Mike was writing the original proposal to the Wallace Foundation that supported this line of work, he didn't invite us to carry out *his* agenda or run the project himself. Instead, he turned to us and several other colleagues and asked, "Where do *you* want to go?" When others doubted our choices to invest in understanding central office leadership, he had our backs. Throughout, he greatly improved the quality of this work, both when he provided feedback and when he remained silent. And he always managed to smile at us, even on our most unpleasant days. For these and other reasons, we are truly grateful.

CHAPTER 1

From Supervision to Support

PRINCIPAL SUPERVISOR JUNE WRIGHT scanned the faces of the four fourth-grade teachers sitting around the table.[1] She wondered how well they were following the conversation that their principal, Michael Maxwell, was leading. Principal Maxwell was trying to share what he saw when he observed their classrooms and help the teachers to discuss the quality of their teaching. He was concerned that math achievement for African American boys in the fourth grade had dipped significantly, and when he visited fourth-grade classrooms he saw the teachers talking with some African American boys in ways that likely contributed to their disengagement. But now the teachers were mostly sharing how the curriculum the central office required was not working for them, how disruptive some students were, and how a few parents were taking up their time with all sorts of complaints.

As part of his professional learning plan that he developed with Principal Supervisor Wright, Principal Maxwell was trying to get better at having such challenging conversations with teachers, but without much success. To supplement Principal Maxwell's efforts to lead his own learning, Principal Supervisor Wright had demonstrated for Principal Maxwell how to have such conversations, showing how to share observational data to paint a detailed picture of the quality of teaching and the implications for the school's equity goals and the experience of individual students. In the process, Principal Supervisor Wright had modeled how to use particular questioning strategies to help teachers honestly and critically consider the quality of their teaching in ways that motivated them to try new approaches. But now that Principal Maxwell was trying those moves himself, teachers were pushing back on the data and avoiding the main discussion points.

At one point, Principal Supervisor Wright turned to Principal Maxwell and interjected, "Principal Maxwell, they are saying that not all the student results are because of the classroom teaching. Maybe they are right. What if you asked them to play out some alternative explanations and discuss their pros and cons? Try keeping them focused on better understanding the problem the data are showing you."

As the discussion continued, Principal Maxwell invited rather than resisted the teachers' various explanations for the student results, and then said, "Now, for just a few minutes let's set aside what we can't control and focus on what we can. Let's assume these data are telling us something we care about that we may not be great at yet. You see me here with my boss helping me do something I'm clearly not great at yet. We all have those things. What do we wonder about how we might be a part of what's going on?"

As the conversation unfolded, one teacher commented, "I didn't even realize that I was blaming students and other things rather than looking at the data to understand what I am doing. And we just had that implicit bias training, right? And here I am, not seeing what I'm not seeing." Another teacher said, "I think I got distracted, because you were saying I was not doing anything for those kids. I know that Myles is a challenge for me, but I don't think that's typical of what I am doing."

Principal Maxwell acknowledged the importance of the group working together to sharpen what they see about their practice. He agreed that he made general comments about the experience of African American boys, based on the school's broad test score trends, but of course each child is different and he and his staff all have to commit themselves to truly seeing each and every student. He said that for his part he would focus the next round of his classroom observations on being even more specific about how the teachers' engagement with individual African American boys may vary in their classrooms and help the teachers make sense of what to do next. He encouraged them to observe one another's practice and think of other evidence they could bring to "really make their teaching visible."

These scenes increasingly play out in school districts across the country: school principals dedicating their time to supporting their teachers' success—especially with students of color, students who qualify for services for English language learners, students from families living in poverty, and other students public school systems have historically underserved—and principal supervisors helping principals learn how to get better at doing so. These scenes bode well for actually improving principal leadership, quality teaching, and student learning.

Educational research continues to reinforce the idea that teaching is the most important school-related influence on student learning and that principals' leadership is essential to helping teachers succeed—a form of principal leadership sometimes called *instructional leadership*.[2] Principals strengthen their instructional leadership when they take intentional steps during their regular workday to learn how to improve that leadership, often alongside others, much like how doctors and other professionals engage in ongoing on-the-job learning with various mentors throughout their careers.[3]

Based in part on such research and their own experience as principals, some district leaders have charged Wright and other principal supervisors with helping their principals learn to lead for excellent classroom teaching for each and every student.[4] By asking principal supervisors to focus their time in this way, district leaders are saying that the job of helping principals grow as instructional leaders is so important to students' success that it should also be the core work of their supervisors. In some smaller districts where the superintendent supervises principals, the superintendents themselves are rethinking how they work to maximize their time and effectiveness supporting principals' instructional leadership.

But when Wright and other principal supervisors dedicate themselves to helping principals grow as instructional leaders, they typically are swimming against the tide of central office "business as usual." While central offices have been around for over a century, only within the past two decades have policy and research begun to emphasize ensuring excellent teaching and learning as a main responsibility of school district central offices—almost a hundred years into central office's history.

Wright's principal certification program was one of the first in the country to emphasize principal leadership for teaching and learning improvement and educational equity specifically. Principal supervisors like Wright describe that when they first started out in the principalship, they were part of the new generation that took leadership for high-quality teaching and learning as a given. They loved classroom teaching and became principals in part to give other teachers the support they wished they had received from their own principals to help each student succeed.

But once they became school principals, they found little time each day to work with their teachers on teaching and learning. Instead, despite their districts' formal emphasis on instruction, too many of their teachers, parents, central office leaders, and community members expected them to be a jack-of-all-trades, ensuring the smooth operation of their school as well as engaging parents, supervising lunch and recess, managing the school budget, dealing with discipline and conduct, and attending school and community events.

The professional development that central offices provided for principals typically reinforced this broad operations and compliance orientation to the role. As a principal, Wright met with other principals about once a month at the central office headquarters downtown as part of her professional development. In those meetings, central office staff delivered information on district policies and procedures, usually concerning operational and compliance matters such as new safety rules, budgeting reporting templates, and graduation requirements. As their districts increased the emphasis on instructional improvement, the meetings promised professional development related to instructional matters. But the sessions still mostly focused on the delivery of information—such as updates on new state instructional standards—and not activities to strengthen principals' ability to lead for high-quality teaching and learning.

Upon their promotion to principal supervisor, leaders like Wright found that principal supervision was cut from the same mold—largely consumed with operations and compliance matters, such as tracking down requests for building repairs and evaluating principals, with little time to support principals' leadership of teaching and learning. For example, when we asked a team of principal supervisors in a midsized district simply, "What is your job?" we filled seven pages of chart paper with comments such as:

Help with staffing
Graffiti removal
Getting coaches for teachers
The high school steering committee
Monitoring implementation of the superintendent's priorities
Parent questions

Principal hiring
Principal evaluation
Sounding board
Email responder
Budget
Conflict mediator

Superintendents in smaller districts who served as principal supervisors also described spending most of their time on community and school board relationships as well as overall district management with very little focus on instruction. One superintendent, with a central office of ten other staff, pulled out his calendar, which showed that in the last week he had attended the football game, fixed budget issues, dealt with a school bus repair, talked with the newspaper about the summer meal program, and met with parents. These superintendents spent a great deal of time with principals in meetings in the central office and in schools generally—engaging with parents and listening to teachers and principals about their successes and concerns—but not working with principals intensively on the quality of their instructional leadership.

These principal supervisors understood that operations, compliance, and principals' instructional leadership were not necessarily mutually exclusive.[5] One explained that particular kinds of budgeting, school staffing models, and strategies for facilities management, for example, are fundamental to excellent teaching and learning; helping principals grow in those areas was important to principals' development as instructional leaders.[6] But too often, principal supervisors do not take an instructional improvement focus to that work, instead mainly helping or telling principals to get budgeting, staffing, and facilities done, rather than supporting their leadership in those areas in ways that foster teaching and learning improvement. Or, principal supervisors end up addressing operational and compliance matters themselves in an effort to free up time for focusing on instructional leadership. But absent other changes in their central offices, that work can become endless and ultimately consume their relationship with their principals.

So, when we say that principal supervisors who focus on principals' growth as instructional leadership are swimming against the tide of central office business as usual, we mean that they are 1) teaching principals how to engage in a relatively recent and fundamental shift in their own role to center their leadership on high-quality classroom teaching and learning, 2) supporting principals' instructional leadership growth in ways that their central office has not traditionally emphasized, and 3) doing so in a role that principals and others throughout their system have counted on for other things.

How are principal supervisors making these promising, but challenging, fundamental shifts? With what results? What conditions help or hinder their progress? This book takes up these questions, which lie at the heart of how school districts are working to ensure excellent teaching and learning for each and every student as part of their broader efforts to address inequitable educational opportunities and outcomes. Our findings come from two systematic, empirical investigations in nine school districts of various sizes where principal supervisors were charged with shifting their focus from mainly operations and compliance to helping principals grow as instructional leaders. (See table 1.1.)

These investigations involved hundreds of hours of real-time observations of principal supervisors working with their principals. We also draw on our experience partnering with school districts across the country over the past decade, helping them use the ideas from the research to redesign principal supervision and otherwise transform their school district central offices into engines of educational equity. (For more on our research study and methods, see the Note on Methodology at the end of the book.)

Using extended cases and detailed examples, we show that some principals grew in their focus on and engagement in instructional leadership, while others either did not or did so despite their principal supervisor. The differences in their principal supervisor's work with them were clearly aligned with these dichotomous results. The principal supervisors in the positive cases took what we call a *teaching*

TABLE 1.1 Study sites

	DISTRICT	APPROXIMATE NUMBER OF STUDENTS DURING STUDY PERIOD	NUMBER OF PRINCIPAL SUPERVISORS IN STUDY/ TOTAL NUMBER OF PRINCIPAL SUPERVISORS IN DISTRICT
Study 1 2007–2008	1A	200,000	14/15
	1B	55,000	5/5
	1C	40,000	6/8
Study 2 2011–2012	2A	50,000	6/6
	2B	19,000	2/2
	2C	2,000	1/1
	2D	5,000	1/1
	2E	5,000	1/1
	2F	3,000	1/1

and learning approach to supporting principals' growth as instructional leaders; they helped principals lead their own learning and mentored them directly using distinct teaching and learning moves such as modeling and differentiation. By contrast, the principal supervisors in the other cases tended to engage in traditional principal supervision with an emphasis on directing, monitoring, and evaluating principals.

We identify specific conditions that district leaders can put in place to increase the chances that their principal supervisors will take a teaching and learning approach over time and grow in their ability to do so. We caution districts about overrelying on outside coaches and instead highlight the importance of district leaders hiring people with the right prior knowledge, positioning the supervisor of principal supervisors as a main support for principal supervisors' growth, and helping principal supervisors lead their own learning.

But first, in the rest of this introductory chapter, we put the work of our nine study districts—and the many others with whom we have worked—in research and historical context. This context illuminates the promise of the districts' initiatives that emphasized principals' growth as instructional leaders as well as the fundamentally new direction these initiatives represented for school district central offices and principal supervisors in particular. We then describe common elements of the district initiatives and how we approached our data collection and analysis to capture implementation as it unfolded in real time. We conclude by summarizing each of the next chapters and highlighting what's ahead in this volume.

Our goals are that, by the end of this chapter, readers will: deepen their appreciation of the importance, promise, and challenge of the reforms in principal supervision our study districts set out to make; understand that the reforms centered instructional leadership as the core of a principal's work and positioned principal supervisors as the main supports for principals' instructional leadership growth; and learn how they might use this volume as a resource for driving deep and meaningful change in their settings, whether they are central office leaders, school principals, policy makers, funders, school support providers, or researchers, among others.

THE PROMISES AND CHALLENGES OF PRINCIPALS' INSTRUCTIONAL LEADERSHIP

District leaders' efforts to focus the principalship on instructional leadership are promising in that they reflect a growing base of research that, over the past two decades, has shown that principals are an important influence on teaching and student learning. For example, Leithwood and colleagues demonstrated that school leadership "is second only to teaching among school-related factors in its impact on student learning."[7] Other studies have associated principals' engagement in instructionally related activities, including defining their school's mission, managing their instructional program, and promoting a positive learning climate, with such results as sustained high student achievement on state test scores.[8] These and other studies suggest that district efforts to focus principals on leading for high-quality teaching and learning bode well for such results.

But calls for principals to operate as able instructional leaders come relatively recently in the history of the principalship and therefore likely pose challenges for districts trying to realize high-quality principal instructional leadership at scale.[9] For much of the history of public schooling, principals have been expected to operate as strong school managers—making sure teachers were licensed, students attended class, cabinets remained stocked, and hallways were safe—not as leaders of teaching quality, let alone the kind of teaching that interrupts centuries-old educational inequities and ensures excellent educational opportunities and outcomes for each and every student.[10] Larry Cuban famously called this dynamic the "managerial imperative," where administrative work overrode other commitments for school leaders, including those related to the quality of teaching and learning.[11]

Only starting in the 1990s did research on the principalship gain steam and begin to identify principals' instructional leadership as a key element in school improvement.[12] In 1996, the Council of Chief State School Officers, the National Governors Association, colleges of education, and school support organizations codified some of this research in the first-ever national standards for principals. These standards defined instructional leadership as including tasks such as setting a widely shared vision for learning, developing a school's culture and instructional program, and managing the school to ensure a safe and effective learning environment for each and every student.[13] And though the federal government significantly increased its role in education starting in the 1960s and 1970s, not until the early 2000s did federal policy make funding available specifically to support the quality and effectiveness of principal leadership for excellent teaching and learning.[14]

So district efforts to define and support the principalship as instructional leadership now have the support of national standards and new funding. But these efforts still come nearly a century into the history of the school principalship. Some principals currently in the role likely were teachers in schools whose principals did not emphasize instructional leadership and participated in principal preparation programs that did not either. Those principals are now being asked to focus their leadership on instruction after many years of preparation and focus elsewhere.

Even if you are a principal who has always understood your role as leading for high-quality teaching and learning, engaging in such leadership is no simple task. Research has come to identify a progressively challenging array of tasks and activities that instructional leadership entails. For instance, this research shows that principals operate as able instructional leaders not just when they foster a positive culture but also when they cultivate a "learning climate" characterized by safety, rigor, and an emphasis on college-going for all students; "program coherence" among the instructional initiatives at a school; and "quality professional development."[15] Early studies called on principals to visit classrooms and observe teaching as a main part of professional development. More recent work clarifies that such observations can support high-quality teaching when they help principals give teachers intentional feedback over time about their strengths and areas for growth in instruction.[16]

Instructional leadership involves fostering the leadership of others—teachers, high school department heads, and other staff—to support the schools' overall approach to teaching and learning improvement.[17] Similarly, principals operate as able instructional leaders when they support teachers working in teams, sometimes called professional learning communities (PLCs), to strengthen the quality of their teaching and student learning.[18] For instance, principals positively influence teachers' participation in PLCs and other teacher teams by shaping a school vision that encourages all teachers to work collaboratively toward school goals and setting up space and time for teachers to collaborate.

Research further suggests that principals operate as able instructional leaders when they not only develop the teachers they have, but also pay careful attention to how they recruit, select, and place teachers to ensure that the teachers are the right fit for both the school and the position.[19] Such leadership often means engaging in "strategic retention," or creating school conditions that encourage a school's most effective teachers to stay and thrive while also helping teachers who are less effective or less of a fit with the school to move on.[20]

More recently, scholars working from a critical race perspective have emphasized the importance of an antiracist, culturally responsive approach to school leadership.[21] When principals take such an approach, they intentionally identify and actively dismantle school practices and systems that have perpetuated educational inequities and rebuild them in ways that center support for students who have historically experienced disparities based on race, class, ability, gender, sexuality, or language and other identity markers.[22] In this view, principals play pivotal roles in continually interrogating and reflecting on how their own racial, gender, and other positionalities influence their leadership, modeling for other staff how to engage in such critical self-reflection, helping teachers use culturally responsive pedagogy and curricula, and forging trusting, honest, and collaborative relationships with families and communities that value each student's cultural strengths.[23]

And despite calls to end the managerial imperative, principals with strong orientations to their role as instructional leaders still struggle to protect their time for instructional matters.[24] For example, in one study such principals talk about being buried in paperwork, including hundreds of emails, and other administrative and largely regulatory demands, and spending considerable time on noninstructional matters such as health screenings.[25]

In sum, district calls for principals to operate as instructional leaders are promising for realizing high-quality teaching and learning districtwide. Yet, due to the relative newness of that emphasis, the various tasks and activities instructional leadership entails, and the persistent demands on principals' time, realizing high-quality principal instructional leadership in individual schools and throughout entire districts poses significant challenges.

WHAT'S THE CENTRAL OFFICE (AND PRINCIPAL SUPERVISORS) GOT TO DO WITH IT?

The leaders of the districts we feature in this book understood the promise of principal instructional leadership. They knew that if their principals were to operate as able instructional leaders, their central offices had to step up and support them in doing do. Some knew well the successes in New York City District #2 in the 1990s, where Superintendent Tony Alvarado and others developed comprehensive supports for principals' instructional leadership, and they took inspiration from that example.[26] But actually providing that support also posed significant challenges for central offices that more typically had little success in promoting teaching and learning improvement generally, let alone principal instructional leadership specifically.

A common refrain in studies of various school improvement efforts—including effective schools, comprehensive school reform, site-based management, school autonomy initiatives, and standards-based reform—is that district central offices interfere with implementation, even in cases where district leaders themselves launched the initiative.[27] In some instances, district central offices got too involved with implementation by placing demands on schools that interrupted their improvement efforts.[28] In others, the district central offices hampered instructional improvement by providing too little oversight, training, and support.[29]

Central office administrators' limited understanding of teaching and learning also has impeded the implementation of various standards-based curriculum reform initiatives across subject matter areas.[30] Long-standing norms in central offices have clashed with initiatives to promote educational equity.[31] Weak and inequitable channels of communication and trust between central offices and schools frustrate school improvement efforts and actually negatively impact a district's lowest performing schools.[32]

Superintendents and other individual central office leaders frequently bear the blame for implementation failures. But these leaders work in central office systems that were not designed to drive instructional improvement in the ways that policy and research now demand or to support principals' instructional leadership specifically. Turning back to history reveals that school district central offices were set up in urban areas at the turn of the last century to handle the "Americanization" of immigrants and bring Progressive Era ideas about the managerial imperative into the running of school systems. Then new federal funding streams for rural schools likewise fueled the creation of school districts to manage finances as well as to raise local funds on which receipt of federal funds was contingent.[33] And over the first half of that century, in tandem with the principalship, school district central offices across the country built up their expertise with basic business functions such as managing enrollments and the regulatory work of ensuring proper teacher licensing and monitoring use of funds and other resources.

As the federal and state funding for math and science as well as particular student populations grew in the 1960s and 1970s, district central offices responded by increasing the number of staff and functions related to teaching and learning. But they typically did so unstrategically, adding staff and programs in a piecemeal fashion. For instance, as Title I funds for "disadvantaged" students became available, central offices generally either created new positions or assigned existing staff to manage those funds. When the Individuals with Disabilities Education Act (IDEA) started to provide funding for schools and districts, central offices likewise added responsibilities, positions, or offices to support it. This process continued as districts became increasingly responsible for funds related to particular curriculum content areas.

Not surprisingly, by the 2000s, central offices of all sizes reflected what we call a "Frankenstein effect." Central offices, generally meaning well, added on functions as resources and policy priorities emerged. But like Frankenstein, they typically lumbered along with little coordination within or across functions and sometimes worked against themselves. For instance, districts can only allocate so much time for teacher professional development. So if you are a central office director of mathematics, you are competing for that finite amount of time against colleagues responsible for Title I, bilingual education, and English language arts, among others in your same Teaching and Learning unit. Different human resources (HR) staff typically handle discrete aspects of personnel processes from hiring to retirements. These functions are often highly specialized with little opportunities for collaboration and leave some teachers and principals feeling like the left hand doesn't know what the right hand is doing.

Recognizing a Systemic Challenge

Leaders in the districts we studied understood these challenges and that the challenges were systemic—so deeply rooted in the institutional fabric of their central offices that typical reform efforts would have limited success. For instance, one director of Teaching and Learning explained that if you think it is okay that every year directors of different curricular and service programs compete with one another for time with teachers, then the district's system for professional development works extremely well; but if you think that those resources should work together to support each and every school well, then the system is fundamentally broken. The head of HR in an urban district said that if you are a school principal who knows which HR staff to call when, then you probably don't have problems with how HR works. But such a system was extremely inequitable, favoring veteran principals with strong ties throughout his department who tended to be in the higher rather than lower performing schools.[34]

In this context, district leaders began to ask: If we are serious about ensuring excellent teaching and learning for each and every student, how can we remove the systemic barriers to those results *within our central office* and proactively support all of our schools? Isn't it fundamentally inequitable that some school principals receive better services and supports from the central office because they know whom to call while others do not?

Redesigning to Support High-Quality Teaching and Learning

Given such concerns, the districts we studied set out to rebuild their *entire* central offices to focus on high-quality teaching and learning districtwide. As one superintendent said, "When I arrived . . . it was clear that our goal had to be nothing less than a total district transformation." In the words of another, "We aim to retool the entire district to support instruction and leadership in the buildings." A third said, "We are really trying to transform the culture of the district and schools . . . [to] focus on instruction . . . It's a shift in their culture . . . saying that's what most important."

One district leader referred to the work as fundamentally "rewiring" each and every central office function to support educational equity. Some of these leaders literally sat down with their staff and a blank chalkboard or poster paper and asked questions such as, "What is the central office that we would build if we could start over from scratch and create an organization whose every fiber works in powerful and coordinated ways to support teaching and learning for each and every student?"

Leaders' new designs for their central offices left no one untouched. One central office leader in a midsized urban district explained that she had "hard conversations" with each and every staff person. She said that if each person could not demonstrate that they contributed to a system of support that led to demonstrable improvements in the quality of teaching, then they needed to rethink their work:

> [Throughout the central office, everyone was required to] sit down and figure out how their job related to student achievement. Each one of us had to do that. And it was very difficult for some people on my staff. I remember my secretary said, "Well, I don't have anything to do with it." I said, "Well, if you don't, then go home . . . Go home and think about it and come back." And so she did and she says, "Well, you know, I did do the [coordination of resources for the school board], and if I don't do it well, then the board gets mad and maybe they won't approve something that the school needs." Bingo—there you go . . . That's our first business: How do we make ourselves relevant to schools?

The superintendent in a small district used a similar strategy. As he explained, "We had a series of meetings last year where I gave all of the district office folks opportunities to think about their job, and what they do here, and its impacts on various things as kind of a baseline model . . . And we did this over about a six- to eight-month period—think about ways that the things they do could help teaching and learning, or hinder it. And for many of them it was kind of the first time of ever even thinking about stuff like that."

An underlying tenet of the transformation efforts in all of the districts was to rebuild every central office function, in tandem, in ways that supported high-quality instructional leadership and teaching and learning in each of their schools. For example, new designs for the Teaching and Learning unit focused on collaboration and impact: helping staff work together to identify selective and strategic—not exhaustive—supports to help each school build on its strengths to realize its school improvement goals. HR leaders called for streamlining and predictability; eliminating unnecessary paperwork, redesigning and automating most transactions to save central office and school staff time, and maximizing staff time on strategic hiring—recruiting teachers and leaders who fit the district's vision and streamlining screening so principals received a manageable, well-selected group of applicants for each position. Operational units such as custodians worked to increase their responsiveness to save principals' and teachers' time on such matters. They also began to design new ways of working to ensure that they contributed to the instructional mission of each school, for example, by identifying ways to enhance the physical space and interacting with students in intentional and positive ways.[35]

Envisioning Principal Supervision as an Anchor and Driver of Central Office Transformation

As part of these central office transformation efforts, district leaders began to shine a particularly bright light on principal supervision. They asked questions such as: What do our principal supervisors do day-to-day? How does doing those things contribute to a system of support for high-quality teaching and learning in each and every school? Isn't the job of helping principals grow as instructional leaders so important that we should make it the main responsibility of the staff to whom they report?

As leaders of midsized to large districts explored these questions, they surfaced what June Wright and other principal supervisors across the country knew well from experience. Namely, principal supervisors with titles such as Assistant Superintendent or Executive Director typically had little interaction with principals around instruction, let alone principals' leadership of instruction. The engagement of these executive-level staff in other central office functions had few if any regular benefits in terms of improving teaching and learning—and actually seemed to take pressure off other central office staff to rethink and improve their core work. And when principal supervisors worked in those ways, they sent the wrong message about their district's commitment to high-quality teaching and learning and the principals' pivotal role in leading for such results.

These district leaders came to view a new principal supervisor–principal relationship as the anchor for their theory of central office improvement. They argued that if principal supervisors focus their time on helping principals grow as instructional leaders, then principals will come to value their own growth in that area as the definition of professional success and, in fact, improve their instructional leadership over time. Looking outward from the principal supervisor role, they also posited that if principal supervisors stop doing various tasks that are actually the responsibility of other central office units, then those other units will face increasing pressure to rethink how they serve schools and more fully engage in the central office transformation process.

In the smaller districts, the superintendent or head of Teaching and Learning generally supervised principals on top of various other responsibilities such as working with the school board and communicating with families and community members. Most superintendents of these smaller systems reported that they began to rethink their central offices in part in response to examples from larger systems, but that they initially struggled to relate to the changes in principal supervision. As one said in an early interview, "We don't have a lot of layers of administrative support, so that [example from a larger district] didn't seem to resonate for a small district." But over time, they realized that the examples about principal supervision applied to how they carried out their role as a superintendent who also supervised principals. These leaders said that given the small size of their central offices, they would not be able to shed their other responsibilities completely, but that they could rethink how they supervise principals to emphasize principals' growth as instructional leaders and dedicate more of their own time to that important work. As one small-district superintendent explained, "You don't want a manager in this [superintendent] role; you do want an instructional leader and initiator . . . I have to focus on quality instruction as the theory of action to get our kids school-transition and college-/work-ready—to get to those ends." Another superintendent explained that he launched central office transformation including principal supervision "because we wanted to shift the focus from the management things to what we were all about, which was teaching and learning. Because we weren't getting the results, and we knew we wouldn't get the results in our school district [unless we worked very differently]."

Elevating and Focusing Principal Supervision

In taking action on these ideas, leaders in the larger districts eliminated the position of Assistant or Associate Superintendent and replaced it with a new executive-level role focused on helping principals grow as instructional leaders. In smaller systems, the superintendents assumed full responsibility for principal supervision and recast their own relationships with school principals from a traditional, top-down supervisory relationship to one in which they worked intensively with principals on their instructional leadership. Their definitions of instructional leadership varied on the margins, but all focused on the importance of principals supporting teachers directly and indirectly to strengthen the quality of their teaching for each and every student.

The new role for principal supervisors included working with principals intensively, one-on-one, in their schools to support their growth as instructional leaders. District leaders also charged principal supervisors with convening principals in groups specifically to help principals learn together how to strengthen their instructional leadership. According to one districtwide professional development plan, the district

> invested heavily in creating small networks of schools, in which principals participate every two weeks in professional development activities led by [principal supervisors] . . . These activities are grounded in a cycle of inquiry, with principals analyzing data from their schools, learning about effective instructional practices, and working with their peers to develop strategies for accelerating student achievement . . . The meetings are designed to develop individual principals' capacity as well as the capacity of the group of principals as their own professional learning community.

To support principal supervisors' success with their new responsibility, the midsized and larger districts reduced the number of principals each principal supervisor oversaw. These leaders argued that while the reforms streamlined principal supervisors' responsibilities, the work of supporting principals' growth as instructional leaders was extremely time-intensive and would be hard to accomplish by any one principal supervisor responsible for more than about fifteen principals. Leaders also paid careful attention to how they grouped principals, with a focus on compositions that seemed particularly conducive to principal learning. Most districts stopped organizing principals into groups based on their attendance-area feeder patterns, with elementary, middle, and high school principals from a geographic area all meeting together, since instructional leadership differs at each school level. Instead, district leaders grouped principals by school level, main schoolwide approach (e.g., experiential learning), or another category that made sense from the standpoint of building a learning community of principals.

In smaller districts, superintendents traditionally convened their principals with other members of their leadership team for meetings that addressed various district matters. With the transformations in principal supervision, these superintendents explored convening just their principals in learning community meetings at rotating schools to focus specifically on their instructional leadership. Other superintendents reassessed the work of their entire leadership team, moving most of the information items into brief written memos, and focusing progressively more of their time on learning together what counts as high-quality teaching and learning and how principals and others can support those results.

As we studied these changes, we sought to determine: To what extent did principal supervisors actually succeed in shifting their roles to focus on principals' growth as instructional leaders? With what results for principals? And what conditions helped or hindered them in the process?

A FRAMEWORK FOR UNDERSTANDING PRINCIPAL SUPERVISORS AS SUPPORTS TO PRINCIPALS' GROWTH AS INSTRUCTIONAL LEADERS

The dynamics of principal supervision, and central office transformation more broadly, are complex, so we needed a framework to focus our attention on how principal supervisors were working with their principals in ways that may have mattered to shifts in principals' leadership (see table 1.2). We knew from research on principal learning that school principals, like other professionals, especially benefit from authentic, sustained, job-embedded professional learning opportunities—those

TABLE 1.2 Teaching and learning approach

TEACHING MOVE	DESCRIPTION
Fostering learners' agency	Moves that help learners operate with progressively more independence or agency in leading their own learning, for example, by assisting learners to: • assess their own proficiency with new practices; • develop and implement their own professional learning plan; and • identify and pursue learning supports on the job.
Joint work moves	Moves that help learners embrace new challenging work as a defined set of practices that they and their colleagues collectively value, for example, by: • using a specific shared definition of the new work as common guides for their growth; and • learning alongside learners and opening up their own practice.
Modeling	Demonstrations of new work practices using metacognitive strategies—explicit explanations of what they are modeling and why.
Talk moves	Forms of talk that engage learners in making sense of what new work entails and how to engage in it, for example, by: • verbally challenging learners' understandings of situations; • offering competing theories about underlying problems and potential solutions; and • prompting learners to question long-standing practices that have not been effective.
Brokering	Bridging moves that connect learners to new ideas, understandings, and other resources to advance their learning. Buffering moves that protect learners from potentially unproductive external interruptions to their learning.
Recognizing all learners as learning resources	Moves that help each learner learn from and teach the others in their learning community, identify as on a trajectory toward mastery, and understand learning as an ongoing developmental process for all.
Differentiation	Moves that meet each learner where they are, for example, by: • using evidence to understand each learner's strengths and areas for growth, and how they vary; and • setting and tailoring assistance in ways that build on learners' strengths to leverage their growth in weaker areas.

available while principals are leading their schools in real time, rather than delivered through workshops outside their regular work.[36] For example, studies of New York City Community School District #2 demonstrate the importance of intentional learning opportunities during the regular workday to help principals grow as instructional leaders.[37] These learning opportunities included monthly principal meetings that were often held at school sites and focused on instruction, as well as individualized coaching "apprenticeships" from their supervisor and other coaches in real time. Community School District #2 principals also benefited from "visitations" other principals' schools so they could learn from one another.[38] Another research team reinforced these findings by showing that job-embedded professional development had a statistically significant relationship with the time principals spent on instructional leadership tasks such as engaging with teachers outside the classroom to improve instruction.[39]

Researchers also underscore the importance of principals having access to differentiated supports—those specifically tailored to their strengths and areas of growth—in both one-on-one settings as well as in groups or PLCs. For example, Anderson and colleagues (2012) highlighted the importance of developing the capacity of principals and their schools to understand and solve their own problems, and of intentionally facilitating principal peer networks for schools to learn from one another.[40]

In light of these important findings and our own experience with leading the learning of school system leaders, we turned to socio-cultural theories of learning as the basis for our conceptual framework, since these theories elaborate the kinds of real-time supports that foster professional growth over time, consistent with principal supervisors' charge to create such conditions for principals.[41] Socio-cultural learning theories also are robust—meaning they rest on many investigations across different settings and professions that show how specific common conditions enable learning. This line of scholarship suggested that those principals in our research who grew as instructional leaders would be those whose supervisors worked in ways consistent with socio-cultural theories of learning. What are those ways?

Socio-cultural learning theory starts from the research-based premise that learners improve their performance with particular target tasks, such as instructional leadership, by *doing*—that is, by performing in real time the target tasks with the support of a mentor who takes what we call a teaching and learning approach. In such an approach, the mentor works with a learner one-on-one and in group settings or "communities of practice" using particular teaching moves; in the process, mentors deepen their own understanding of the target task and how to engage in progressively better mentoring. Teaching moves include practices that foster learners' agency over their own learning, "joint work" moves, modeling, talk moves, brokering, recognizing all learners as learning resources, and differentiation. Next we explain each of these moves as a preview of the practices we expected to see principal supervisors engaging in as they helped their principals grow as instructional leaders. Because these ideas distinguished principal supervisors in the positive and negative cases, we use them in the following three chapters to organize our findings.

Fostering learners' agency. Mentors support learning in one-on-one and group settings when they intentionally help learners operate with progressively more independence or agency in leading their own learning.[42] Through leading their own learning, learners develop self-regulating behaviors that help them actively make sense of the new work, without which their behavior will not change in meaningful ways.[43] Such self-regulating behaviors prompt learners to continue to practice and seek out help with the new work even when the mentor is not present. Agency for learning seems especially important in the context of the school principalship, since principals spend most of their time working without mentors in their individual schools and therefore likely need strong, internal models of the new work or "target tasks" to fall back on.

Mentors reinforce learners' agency over their own learning through such strategies as helping learners assess their own proficiency with a target task, using that experienced-based data to identify and pursue learning supports on their own, and continuously monitoring their own progress.[44] Mentors also model how to learn while doing—for instance, by showing learners strategies they use themselves to connect with learning supports.

Joint work moves. Joint work moves are those that help learners embrace new challenging work, such as instructional leadership, as a defined set of practices that they and their colleagues collectively value. Such moves include principal supervisors' efforts to help their principals use a specific, shared definition of instructional leadership as a guide for their growth. Joint work moves may also include principal supervisors dedicating their own time to principals' growth as instructional leaders and learning alongside them in the process—to reinforce that principals' growth as instructional leaders is their shared valued outcome.[45]

This complex idea often makes intuitive sense to practitioners who know from experience that they are more likely to deepen their engagement in new work practices if they have a progressively clearer sense of the new work and if they see that their success at that work is important not just to themselves but to colleagues and the collective good of their organization.

When their mentors are learning alongside them in a reciprocal manner, learners increase their motivation to learn and also build trust with their mentors through repeated interactions and their mentors' opening up their own practice for growth.

This conception of trust differs from some other treatments that call for building trust as a precondition for change.[46] In the sociocultural view, trust is situational; that is, learners need to trust their mentors not generally but specifically as guides for learning the new target practice. Such trust gets built not in advance but over time as learners work with mentors to deepen their engagement in the particular new work.

Modeling. Mentors support learning when they model or demonstrate the target tasks in practice rather than, for example, talking about those practices in a lecture-like manner or directing people to participate in them.[47] By observing demonstrations, learners develop "a conceptual model of the target task"—literally a mental picture of what it would look like if they were, in this case, exercising instructional leadership in a particular setting that they can emulate.[48] Such conceptual models also provide "an interpretive structure for making sense of the feedback, hints, and connections" from the target task and an "internalized guide for the period when the apprentice is engaged in relatively independent practice."[49] In other words, a model allows learners to ask themselves questions important to their learning, such as, "Based on the images of instructional leadership I can picture in my mind, how should I act in this case?" Or, "Does what I am doing resemble the models of instructional leadership that I have seen, and how can I adjust what I am doing to get closer to the model or intentionally deviate from it?"

Models are particularly powerful learning guides when mentors demonstrate the target tasks and also explain what they are doing and why—moves sometimes called *metacognitive strategies* or "making thinking visible."[50] Such strategies help learners look for the right things during a demonstration. These strategies also allow learners to hear what their mentor is thinking as he performs a particular task, which is important to deepening their understanding of the task and how to perform it.

Talk moves. As the discussion of metacognitive strategies suggests, certain kinds of talk enables learning at deep levels.[51] When mentors and learners verbally challenge each other's understandings of situations and offer competing theories about underlying problems and potential solutions, they increase the individual and collective knowledge they bring to bear on situations important to constructing new mental models of their day-to-day work.[52] Such talk moves include those that prompt learners to see and question their long-standing practices that have not been effective, such as when a principal supervisor asks a principal, "How do you know that the way you engage with teachers is helping improve the quality of student learning in classrooms? What's your evidence?" Such talk moves also prompt learners to actively make sense of new ideas and how to integrate them into their practice, such as when a principal supervisor explores with a principal what instructional leadership moves might help particular teachers improve student engagement and the rigor of classroom tasks.

Brokering. Mentors also assist with learning by brokering or strategically bridging learners to and buffering them from outside influences.[53] *Bridging* involves bringing new ideas, understandings, and other resources into the community in ways that advance participants' learning. Absent such infusions of outside influences, participants can become isolated or repeat old patterns in ways that make them passive rather than active learners.

Bridging can be particularly effective when a mentor actively translates, tailors, or otherwise curates the resources to ensure they support the learners in their specific contexts. Translation involves, for example, not simply passing along a new book or article to learners but framing why the resource may be helpful and possibly offering specific reflection questions to focus the reading and time to discuss it with colleagues and apply it to their work. Similarly, a mentor might work with an outside guest in advance to ensure that how the guest works with the group is especially likely to serve as a learning resource.

On the flip side, *buffering* involves shielding learners from potentially unproductive external interruptions to their learning.[54] Especially in complex work environments, opportunities for learning can get put off as tasks emerge with the promise of more immediate results. Buffering not only protects learning time but also reinforces for learners that—especially since it can take time for learning efforts to produce results—learners must consistently prioritize protection of their learning time themselves.

Recognizing all learners as learning resources. Sometimes important learning resources *within* a group of learners go untapped because learners do not know one another's strengths or see one another as learning resources. Mentors enable learning when they recognize each learner as important and valuable to the learning of others in the community and help each community member learn from and teach the others.[55] Such efforts increase the learning resources available to learners by helping them see the resources right under their own noses. In addition, when a mentor recognizes a learner as a resource for others, that learner comes to see herself as on her way to becoming more expert in particular work practices—a form of identity development important to realizing ambitious performance goals.

In recognizing the value of all learners, mentors actively resist fixed definitions of "expertise" as an individual trait or an ability that a learner has across tasks.[56] Rather, they view expertise as always in development and variable by task. As an example of the latter, a principal supervisor would not view a given principal as an overall expert in instructional leadership. Instead, the supervisor would distinguish that, for example, the principal is advanced in certain aspects of instructional leadership such as providing teachers with feedback or leading school improvement planning but more novice at designing professional development for teachers. The supervisor would then help the principal build on his strengths to grow in his weaker areas and do so continuously—because growth is a process, not a destination.[57]

Differentiation. Learners' abilities to engage in target tasks differ and mentors support learners' growth when they meet each learner where she is and tailor assistance to her particular strengths and areas for growth.[58] Mentors differentiate for these and other learners by first using evidence to understand those specific differences and how they vary by setting, since people who can engage in a task at a high level in one context may not be able to do so in another one.[59] Differentiation that supports growth also proceeds from a strengths-based approach—deepening learners' engagement in their growth areas as a strategy to support their development in weaker areas.

Markers of Learning

According to socio-cultural learning theories, learning involves the progression from novice to more expert practice.[60] But how would we know if principals and their supervisors were progressing in their instructional leadership and a teaching and learning approach to support it? We adapted Grossman and colleagues' (1999) "degrees of appropriation" scale to make such distinctions because it, too, uses socio-cultural learning theories about stages of typical progression from novice to expert practice—in this case, the depth to which principals' practice reflected instructional leadership and the depth to which principal supervisors' practice was consistent with taking a teaching and learning approach.[61] Figure 1.1 represents these distinctions.

According to this scale, learners begin as novices who have not yet begun to talk about their practice or engage in practices consistent with the new ways of working. As novices progress, they first will talk about their practices in ways consistent with the new ways of working but still engage in the old ways of working in practice. These learners are not trying to be deceitful. Instead, novices' limited understanding of what the new work involves can lead them to misunderstand the degree to which they are already engaging in the new ways of working.[62] David Cohen captured this phenomenon in the classic case of Mrs. Oublier, a classroom teacher who had to implement ambitious new standards for teaching mathematics. Mrs. Oublier genuinely believed her practice was reflecting those standards when her practice actually demonstrated that she did not understand the difference between familiar strategies and what the new standards demanded.[63]

As learners continue to practice using the new ideas, their work may reflect their engagement with the new ideas at a surface level. At this stage, learners' practice begins to reflect the new ways of working, but not regularly, and learners still mostly work in the old ways. These learners begin to express some understanding of the new work and why to engage in it.

With further practice, learners engage with understanding—their practice often reflects what the new work entails and why to engage in it. After working at this level over time, learners may reach "mastery"—a state of practice at which they engage with understanding across multiple contexts and years. At mastery, a learner can improvise—create new ways of working consistent with but beyond the once-new ideas, such that they improve on the repertoire of practice itself in ways that contribute to progressively more powerful results.

Supportive Conditions

Socio-cultural learning theories led us to hypothesize that principal supervisors would also benefit from the kinds of mentoring we just

FIGURE 1.1 Degrees of appropriation

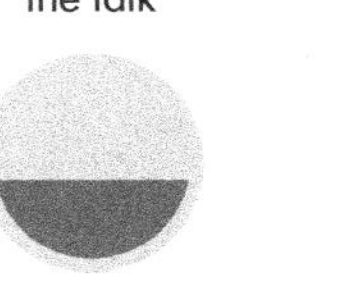

Not adopting	Adopting the talk	Engaging at a surface level	Engaging with understanding	Mastery
Does not yet talk about their practice or engage in practices consistent with the new work.	Talks about their practice in ways consistent with the new work, but actual practice does not yet reflect it.	Practice begins to reflect the new work, but does not yet demonstrate deep understanding of which practices are consistent with it or why to engage in those practices.	Practice often reflects the new work and demonstrates deepening understanding of what practices are consistent with it and why to engage in those practices. Practices consistent with the new work are a regular part of daily practice.	Practice routinely reflects the new work at the level of "engaging with understanding" across multiple contexts and years. Practice across settings and over time demonstrates ability to improvise—to develop new ways of working likely to contribute to progressively more powerful results.

highlighted. We hypothesized that such assistance likely would not yet be available within central offices, given the newness of central office transformation and the reforms of the principal supervisor role specifically. Perhaps as a result, all our study districts had been working with an outside organization to support them with the transformation process and to provide professional development to principal supervisors. Research in education suggested that these arrangements boded well; outside organizations, sometimes called *intermediaries*, can bring important expertise into a school district, especially to support the implementation of new partnership relationships with schools and new ideas about teaching and learning.[64]

Prior knowledge also matters in terms of how assistance relationships and communities of practice play out. Such knowledge is not simply a function of experience or years of service; rather, it emphasizes that professionals approach situations with particular mental models or frames that help them understand what is happening and what they should do. For instance, Mrs. Oublier interpreted the new mathematics standards in light of her existing frame or mental model and, otherwise uninterrupted, basically continued working as she always had. Extensive training and work experiences of particular kinds can shape a person's prior knowledge, but sometimes fewer, yet profound, experiences can as well. Since frames tend to be taken for granted, they often become apparent not through leaders' self-reports but as leaders make decisions in real time about how to approach particular situations.

OVERVIEW OF THE BOOK

In the rest of this volume, we use these ideas to organize and explain our findings about how principal supervisors went about their work and the conditions that mattered to how they did so. Here, as in all our research and partnerships with school districts, we take a strengths-based approach, focusing on districts where principal supervisors were likely to be successful and seeking to understand how they understood and carried out their challenging charge. We do not evaluate individual principal supervisors, but offer lessons we learned from and with them as they worked with principals in ways more or less consistent with that charge. We provide examples from our study districts and also those from our partner districts where we think the latter illustrate our research findings in ways particularly useful to practitioners.

As we will elaborate in the coming chapters, the crux of what we found is that our conceptual framework got it right. As socio-cultural learning theories suggest, principal supervisors who worked from a teaching and learning approach—either consistently or more often and better over time—were those whose principals demonstrated positive outcomes such as spending time on instructional leadership and handling progressively more challenging instructional leadership work over time. Other principal supervisors engaged in traditional forms of principal supervision—including monitoring, compliance, and supporting operational matters—either consistently or increasingly over the study period, and their principals did not demonstrate engagement or growth in instructional leadership. In some cases, those principals reported that their supervisor actually impeded their focus on instructional leadership. The difference between these two groups was stark and consistent.

Chapter 2 elaborates how principal supervisors in the positive cases took a teaching and learning approach while working with principals one-on-one, and chapter 3 describes how they did so while leading principal PLCs. We show that across both of these settings, these principal supervisors helped principals lead their own learning through such strategies as developing and implementing formal professional learning plans. The principal supervisors supplemented these plans with one-on-one visits with principals and how they led the principal meetings. We share specific examples of the teaching and learning moves principal supervisors made in those settings, including modeling and talk moves to support principals' growth as instructional leaders. Throughout, we also offer some examples of principal supervisors in the negative cases to highlight differences between the teaching and learning approach and traditional principal supervision, as well as to illustrate specific practices principal supervisors would do well to actively avoid.

In chapter 4, we explore why some principal supervisors persisted and grew in taking a teaching and learning approach to their work with principals while others assumed a more traditional supervisory stance, either consistently or over time. Prior knowledge clearly mattered to these results. Surprisingly, we did not associate high-quality outside coaching with positive results—and actually saw no changes in principal supervisors' practice when principal supervisors participated in the higher-quality outside coaching. Instead, we show that supervisors of principal supervisors played key roles in coaching principal supervisors themselves and helping them protect their time and connect to other resources important to their success. Principal supervisors in the positive cases also led their own learning—by making time to learn from and with colleagues and protecting their own time—in ways that help them persist and grow in taking a teaching and learning approach. We remind readers that each district aimed to recast principal supervision as one part of a broader effort to transform its central office into a driver of educational equity. The districts likely would not have seen the success with principal supervision that they did absent those broader changes.

This work offers some clear directions for leaders, policy makers, researchers, and others who seek to similarly elevate the school principalship and district central offices as main drivers of educational equity. In chapter 5, we elaborate some of those directions. These recommendations encourage school district leaders to recognize the pivotal role principal supervisors can play in a districtwide system that supports high-quality teaching and learning for each and every student. Doing so successfully does not involve adding support for principal instructional leadership onto principal supervisors' already loaded plates. District leaders must fundamentally recast their traditional principal supervisory function, and support for it, so that a teaching and learning approach to helping principals grow as instructional leaders is at its core. In the process, district leaders should heed the example of these pioneering districts that understood the shifts in principal supervision as part of a broader strategic effort to transform their outmoded central office into a driver of educational equity.

Policy makers, funders, and others can help by encouraging this work and strategically investing in central office leadership for school improvement. Such investments could initially focus on principal supervision but will not see success with that strategy absent support for deeper shifts throughout the central office.

School principals and their success in ensuring their teachers and students grow and thrive is ultimately what the findings in this volume are all about. In chapter 5, we also discuss the importance of principals starting to let go of what in some cases are well-developed and well-justified strategies for limiting their engagement with their supervisor and central office. School principals can be main agents of positive change in their supervision by understanding how their principal supervisor could support them through a teaching and learning approach and opening themselves up to that new relationship. Principals could also put important pressure on the central office to change by suspending their work-arounds—including not asking their supervisors to help with staffing, operations, and other matters. Such pressure can come in the form of escalating examples of both helpful and disappointing central office performance beyond their supervisors and to their superintendent or others in a position to lead a broader central office transformation.

The book concludes with an appendix that provides specific tools principal supervisors can use to support their own growth in the ways we discuss here. These tools include performance standards to help principal supervisors and their own supervisors track their growth and help principals and central office colleagues understand what to expect of their principal supervisors (exhibit 1). We share items district leaders can use to develop surveys that capture information about principal supervisors' work that is important to their growth (exhibit 2). The Professional Growth Planning tool (exhibit 3) guides principal supervisors in using their performance standards to lead their own learning in ways vital to their success.

We also hope this volume will serve as a useful tool for principal supervisors and their principals to help them see and understand examples of principal supervision in practice to which they may aspire.

To support that process, we tried to maximize examples throughout this book. In exhibit 4, we offer reflection and discussion questions that principal supervisors, principals, and others could use to deepen their engagement with the findings and examples in each chapter.

In that spirit, we begin by introducing Principal Bernice Johnson. Principal Johnson's story represents the kind of experiences principals had with their supervisors when their supervisors worked with them from a teaching and learning approach at a high level.

CHAPTER 2

Teaching and Learning One-on-One

PRINCIPAL BERNICE JOHNSON hangs up the phone after talking with a parent and asks her office manager to do her best to handle all other calls for the rest of the morning. She laughs to herself, remembering how only last year she felt like she had a sign around her neck that read, "Complain to me. The principal is always in!" But with the help of her principal supervisor, Michelle Davis, she has turned her calendar upside down. Last year, despite her best intentions, she spent very little time with her teachers. Now, for about 60 percent of her week, Principal Johnson supports her teacher leadership team in planning for and implementing teacher professional learning opportunities, meets with smaller groups of teachers to talk about the quality of their teaching and how to improve, and provides feedback to individual teachers. Principal Johnson recalled:

> Rebalancing my time was *tough*. There are parent questions, finding out where is that facilities request I put in, recess time, meetings downtown. Michelle asked me some hard questions in my one-on-ones like, "Why are you doing that? What are you *not* doing? What message

> are you sending to your staff about what you value?" Yes, that one got me going because I am all about my students and teachers and I didn't really step back and see I wasn't walking my talk. My values. The phone rings. The fires start. One thing leads to another, and you are in your office dealing with this one student all day or whatever else.

At the beginning of the school year, Principal Supervisor Davis helped Principal Johnson look at her own strengths and areas for growth as an instructional leader and develop a learning plan to follow throughout the year to lead her own learning. As part of the plan, Principal Johnson kept a log of the time she spent on various tasks and blocked off time at the end of each week to review how much time she spent on instructional leadership. She arranged to meet with two other principals who had well-developed teacher leadership teams to learn from their examples. The plan also included working with Principal Supervisor Davis a few days each month on helping teachers use samples of student work as evidence of their teaching quality. Johnson explained:

> We had a real problem with rigor. Our students test well. But when I visit classrooms I see low-level tasks—mostly in the third grade—and teachers asking lower-level questions of our native Spanish speakers. Michelle helped me think about how to use the teacher teams to look more deeply at student work with an implicit-bias lens. She comes to some of those meetings, observes me working with the teams, and gives me feedback. That's something I need and that she's really good at, so when we work together that's our focus.

Principal Johnson explained that her relationship with Principal Supervisor Davis was dramatically different from those with her past supervisors:

> Since time immemorial we've had goal setting meetings with our supervisor in September. And sometimes we would get coaches, but they would come and go. And maybe we look at the goals again at the end of the year. Now, I start every year looking at my own practice, really reflecting. Then I set some goals and work with Michelle to write up a learning plan to help me get to those goals. When she comes out, it's really focused. She's really good with teacher feedback. She

connects me with other principals so I can learn from them. She takes all our learning plans and uses them to plan out our principals' meetings. It's a partnership. It really helps me grow in the right ways.

Over the year and a half we observed them, school principals like Bernice Johnson demonstrated positive results related to their instructional leadership that they attributed to their principal supervisor.[1] First, our data showed that they typically spent more time working with their teachers on instructional matters than they had in the past. For example, one principal described how early in his work with his principal supervisor, the two started out like Johnson and Davis, by identifying conditions that took the principal's time away from instructional leadership. They found that budgeting, while ultimately the principal's responsibility, was where the principal was spending too much time due to problems with the district's online platform and the principal handling basic transactions that could be managed by his office assistant. The principal supervisor brought in another central office staff person to fix the system and the principal adjusted his office staffing. These shifts helped the principal recover hours each week, which he redirected to work that directly related to the improvement of teaching and learning, starting with strengthening his school leadership team to improve how the school used its dedicated professional development time.

At the end of the year, the principal showed us a "data room" he and his teachers had created for teachers to post and track milestones in test scores, grades, and the quality of student work for the school community to reflect on and celebrate. He explained that on the one hand what we were seeing was just a room with lots of paper on the walls. But on the other hand, the room represented the work he and his teachers were able to do together that year, building their collective trust to open up their practice and push for their own growth.

These principals also expressed deepening understanding of the importance of instructional leadership and what it entailed, and we observed them engaging in progressively more complex instructional leadership tasks over time. For some principals, the shift was remarkable. For instance, one principal shared that in the past he had spent very little time on instructional improvement other than hiring good teachers. But he has come to understand how important it is for even those "good teachers" to be intentional about continuous improvement, and it was his work to support that growth and not delegate it or simply hire and hope for it.

Other principals already operated as instructional leaders, but said they had long done so *despite* their principal supervisor and the professional development sessions their central office required them to attend. With the transformation of the principal supervisor role, their supervisor now provided them with feedback, including encouragement, that helped them take the next step in their instructional leadership growth. For instance, one said that she used to dread visits from her principal supervisor, seeing them as taking time away from her focus on instruction. Now, this principal reported, "we look forward to them coming. We welcome their visits and the feedback. And each time we push in a little deeper." Another principal already skilled at instructional leadership reflected, "This is one of the first times [since I have been in this district] that we [all of the principals] are all pulling the rope in the same direction" to lead for instructional improvement. And a principal in another district reported that in the past, when she wanted help with teaching and learning matters she did her best to find support on her own, but struggled to find the time and sometimes felt like she was holding steady rather than getting better. Now, she said, "My [principal supervisor] is who I go to. That's it."

In our analyses, we identified these principals as the "positive" cases due to their reported and demonstrated growth and persistent engagement in instructional leadership practices. We associated some principals with "negative" results since they did not report or demonstrate growth as instructional leaders. Most of the principals in the latter group ended up where Principal Bernice Johnson began—spending most of their time responding to parents, central office staff, and other demands, with little time left for instructional leadership.

Some of these principals said that their principal supervisor mainly evaluated them or helped them with operational issues, that they did not expect their supervisor to do otherwise, and that, given inefficiencies throughout the central office, they appreciated the supervisor's help with operational matters. But most of the principals in the negative examples expressed significant frustration with their principal supervisor for not helping them grow as instructional leaders. For example, one principal reported that he was looking forward to having a principal supervisor who was "more of a thought partner" with him in his growth as an instructional leader but said that is "not the reality right now."

Research findings are not always this clear-cut, but in our studies the differences in results for principals were striking. With little variation, the principals we sampled generally fit these definitions of positive and negative cases. Those in the positive cases generally worked with the same principal supervisors and the principals in the negative cases shared a different group of principal supervisors.

What, more specifically, are these differences in principal supervision between the positive and negative cases?

TEACHING AND LEARNING VERSUS TRADITIONAL SUPERVISION IN ONE-ON-ONE WORK WITH PRINCIPALS

As we described in chapter 1, socio-cultural learning theories suggested that the principals who reported and demonstrated positive results would be those whose principal supervisors worked from a teaching and learning approach. And, in fact, that's what we found: when meeting with their principals one-on-one in their schools or other settings, principal supervisors like Michelle Davis took a teaching and learning approach—and grew in doing so or sustained that way of working over time. Specifically, these principal supervisors:

- helped principals lead their own learning instead of positioning themselves as the main leader of principals' learning; and
- used specific teaching and learning moves, rather than those that foster task completion and compliance in ways that can interfere with professional growth.

Principals in the negative cases worked with principal supervisors whose practice consistently or increasingly reflected the flip side—a more traditional approach focused on operational matters, doing for principals rather than helping principals do for themselves, and compliance. In the rest of this chapter, we elaborate on those distinctions.

Helping Principals Lead Their Own Learning

Principal supervisors in the positive cases made intentional moves to help principals exercise agency or ownership over their learning. As we note in our conceptual framework, when learners *lead their own learning* they tend to access learning supports that are particularly relevant to their strengths and areas for growth and that they can access throughout their regular workday, rather than mainly at specific times or separate from their daily work. Engaging actively in such learning opportunities helps them realize deep shifts in their practice. By contrast, when learning opportunities are *provided to* learners, learners can become passive, tend not to make meaning of new ideas, and, therefore, ultimately not use them (not adopting) or say they are using them without actually doing so in practice (adopting the talk).

Principal supervisors in the positive cases intentionally helped principals lead their own learning using several common strategies. For one, these principal supervisors supported principals in conducting *systematic self-assessments* of their instructional leadership and using those assessments to develop and implement explicit learning plans that emphasized principals as main agents of their own learning. In one such case, a principal supervisor routinely started the year with each principal sharing evidence of his or her leadership along each of the district's formal standards for principals' instructional leadership. The principal and supervisor then used those self-assessments to identify strengths and areas for growth and develop specific plans that the principals would execute to lead their own learning. To supplement the supports the principals could access themselves, the two then included a role for the principal supervisor in the learning plan, including prescheduled meetings throughout the year for the principal and supervisor to check on their progress.

Some principal supervisors adapted the district's evaluation system to help support principals in leading their own learning. For instance, one principal supervisor reported that when he was a principal, he received scores on his evaluation at the end of the year with a couple of suggestions for areas of improvement but little guidance on what to do to actually get better in those areas. As a principal supervisor, he aimed to shift how his principals experienced their evaluation, from a summary of work to a guide for learning that principals valued and actively used.

In his adapted evaluation process, this principal supervisor met with each of his principals at the start of the year to discuss what the evaluation would say if conducted at that point in time. The principal supervisor explained that completing a draft of the evaluation at the start of the year, rather than the end, meant that he could focus his time on the principals' growth instead of evaluation since the principals already knew their scores unless they improved over the year. His principals chose two or three aspects of their leadership as their focus for the year, identified concrete steps to support their growth, and planned to collect evidence of their progress. Then, the end-of-year meetings focused on how well principals had led their own learning, and any changes in evaluation results.

Principal supervisors in the positive cases also *modeled for principals* how to lead their own learning. In one instance, a principal supervisor explained to her principals that her own area for growth that year was to stop spending most of her time directly coaching principals and to focus more on helping principals lead their own learning. Her learning plan included readings she would do with her principals on adult learning and documenting her one-on-one meetings with principals so she could reflect on ways her practice in those meetings demonstrated whether or not she was making progress. A second principal supervisor routinely concluded his visits with principals by writing down what specific steps his principals would take before his next visit and what he himself would do to grow. Another principal supervisor, who characterized himself as having a steep learning curve when it came to knowledge of high-quality instruction, regularly shared with principals during one-on-one meetings that he was "learning too" and asked them to identify aspects of their leadership on which he could provide feedback while also learning from their often more advanced knowledge.

Third, principal supervisors also helped principals *access additional resources* to help them lead their own learning—a form of bridging. For example, one principal supervisor had a principal who struggled to focus his learning for the year. The principal was overwhelmed by the school's multiple challenges and was not sure where to start—either with the school's improvement efforts or his own growth as an instructional leader. The principal supervisor assembled a team of central office staff to help, explaining, "The first week of September we did a school . . . blitz site visit and spent about two and a half hours in there, going into classrooms looking for evidence of teaching and learning, [and then we] gave the principal some feedback." The Director of Teaching and Learning elaborated, "We'll go in. We'll observe. We'll see what we see . . . give you some options, and you can decide what you want to do. I saw that as exactly the role that we should be playing. So I had all the managers there. I spent a full morning walking class to class with the principal."

Some of these principal supervisors also bridged principals to each other as learning resources. For instance, one encouraged a principal to visit a neighboring school, rather than travel across country for expensive training, to deepen his understanding of instructional leadership specifically in literacy. She said, "I'm like a matchmaker. I love helping my principals get to know each other that way."

Even in the smaller districts where all the principals worked together relatively frequently on their district leadership team and in other settings, the principal supervisors in the positive cases created new connections among them to support their learning. For instance, during one school visit, a principal supervisor suggested that the principal contact another principal who already had demonstrated a strong ability to help teachers use the district's new definition of high-quality teaching. At one point during the visit, he said to the principal

> Why don't you call [the other principal]? . . . Ask her to explain to you the whole cycle of taking one group and exposing them to . . . learning targets. Tell her how you went out and visited four or five classrooms and came back and spent forty minutes talking through a reflective process and have her walk you through hers. At the end you may say, "I can do this on my own." You may say, "[Can you] do this with us this first time?". . . Once you get a few cycles under your belt and you jump into the other dimensions, it'll be a lot easier.

By contrast, the principal supervisors in the negative cases typically continued long-standing practices of requiring principals to set goals for the start of each year and reported that they did so because of state requirements. The goals we sampled from their principals tended to focus on students' and teachers' growth, such as:

- Improved reading scores for key student subgroups in fourth grade
- More use of standards to guide instruction across grade levels
- Improved collaboration in teacher learning communities

While these outcomes may result from principals strengthening their instructional leadership, they are not *principal* growth goals—targets for progress in how they lead day-to-day. None of these principals reported that their principal supervisor prompted them to move beyond setting goals to thinking through what they would do throughout the year to support their own learning toward those goals.

Some principal supervisors in the negative cases seemed to actively interfere with principals leading their own learning by telling them where to focus, or sometimes not helping them focus at all. For example, one principal supervisor shared that one of her principals had been unsuccessful at raising test scores at her school. She explained that the problem is clearly lack of student engagement. She told the principal that her focus for the year would be on demonstrating growth in supporting teachers to strengthen student engagement.

In another example, during a professional development session for principal supervisors, a coach asked one of the participating supervisors to describe the main learning focus for one of his principals. The principal supervisor produced many pages of notes from goal-setting meetings, reflecting that he knew he should help principals focus their learning but not how to do so. He read from his documents that the principal's one area of focus included "Quality teaching: planning and preparation, classroom environment, and instruction. Professional development: led by [principal] . . . Decisions made by assessment data. Developing trust, facilitating collaboration, and communication/messaging." Other session participants pushed back, saying, "It's too many pages" and "If I'm a principal, I would have a big picture [from the many topics you listed], but it's hard for me to see with these questions . . . what's the focus?"

In sum, principal supervisors in the positive cases made specific, proactive moves to help principals exercise agency over their own learning as instructional leaders. These moves stood in sharp contrast to those of the principal supervisors in the negative cases who, for example, engaged principals in goal setting without actually helping them develop or focus on goals for their own growth or use them throughout the year to support their growth.

Using Teaching and Learning Moves

When principal supervisors in the positive cases went into a school or other setting and worked with their principals individually, they tended to use teaching and learning moves consistent with our conceptual framework. The principal supervisors in the negative cases worked with their principals less frequently and, when they did, typically took a directive or other approach that reflected limited understanding of the teaching and learning moves.

Joint work moves. To elaborate, as principal supervisors in the positive cases worked with their principals one-on-one, they frequently made moves consistent with joint work, demonstrating that they valued principals' growth as their main professional goal—one they *shared* with their principals. As one principal supervisor expressed, "I help principals realize that the more they're in classrooms, the easier their job gets." Another said, "I spend time helping the principals focus their work—working on the quality of teaching and learning, looking at the student work, looking at the rigor, looking at best practices . . . [Otherwise] it's not going to pay out in dividends in student achievement." According to a third, "So now we're working with . . . principals . . . to really own this [their growth as instructional leaders] . . . That's the work. That's the focus for us. Not walking around a building and making recommendations."

These principal supervisors reinforced the value of their principals' growth as instructional leaders by underscoring that such growth was also *their professional goal and that they were partners* in the effort. To revisit an example we used earlier as a case of modeling how to lead your own learning, one principal supervisor typically concluded one-on-one meetings with his principals by discussing next steps both for the principal and for himself in support of that principal's growth. Several principal supervisors wrote these next steps in emails that they viewed as formal agreements between themselves and their principals about how each party would help the principal realize his or her learning goals.

In another case, a principal had identified supporting inquiry-based mathematics instruction as an area of growth and the principal supervisor shared that she was not especially knowledgeable about such instruction. The principal supervisor suggested that she and the principal work together to grow in that area. She then arranged visits with a mathematics coach from the Teaching and Learning unit who guided them in observing instruction during mathematics lessons and providing feedback to teachers on the extent of their inquiry-based approach.

By contrast, the principal supervisors in the negative cases visited schools infrequently and, when they did, they tended to check up on principals rather than work alongside them in ways consistent with a joint work approach. For instance, one principal supervisor routinely visited schools without notice, observed classrooms, and sent an email to the principal about what she saw and what the principal should do next. Another principal reported, when she asked their principal supervisor for assistance, "I rarely got responses." The principal explained this lack of responsiveness as reflecting how their supervisor did not value their growth as an instructional leader: "I think it's just like most things, particularly in education. You get too many fires to put out, too many other priorities. And so I just got the sense that [my supervisor] had other priorities to deal with other than working directly with me or [my school]."

Some principal supervisors in the negative cases seemed to conflate joint work moves—which are about building collective value around a target practice to propel learning—with whether or not their principals trusted or liked them generally or with simply working together. For instance, when a group of principal supervisors was talking about the research on joint work, one commented that he knew he had the right relationships with his principals because they would call him for anything. A colleague asked how that served as evidence that the principals saw their supervisor as a main partner in their growth as an instructional leader. The principal supervisor simply reiterated, "If they need something, they will call me."

Some of the principal supervisors in the negative cases also thought that they communicated the high value they placed on principals' growth as instructional leaders simply by visiting their school. However, principal reports suggested they viewed the visits differently. For instance, one principal supervisor recounted all the classroom observations he had conducted as evidence that he was continuously reinforcing the value of principals' growth as instructional leaders. But one of his principals described him as regularly "stopping by" to talk with her about what he was seeing in classrooms "because of the location" of his office in her school, not because he particularly valued her work with teachers.

Modeling. Modeling serves as an important resource for learning by providing learners with examples that they can emulate when engaging in complex work. Models are especially strong learning supports when those doing the modeling use metacognitive strategies of naming what they are doing and why—to help learners not just go through the motions but develop an understanding of what the models are doing and why they are important. Earlier we noted that principal supervisors in the positive cases modeled for principals how to lead their own learning. These principal supervisors also frequently modeled for principals how to engage in specific instructional leadership tasks or activities, and used intentional metacognitive strategies in the process.

As one principal supervisor explained, some principals were "stumped" by how to improve teaching quality and many "need to see a model in action" to understand how to lead for such results. In another principal supervisor's words, "I recognize that there's a delicate balance between what I know and what they need to know. And so *telling* them is really not an effective method." This principal supervisor continued, "Ultimately, when I leave I want them to know how to do it," and simply telling them what to do will not achieve that result. Another explained, "If I'm going to have any impact at all on these schools, I have to teach them—and teach them *why* we're doing what we're doing and what makes a difference and help them to become instructional leaders." This principal supervisor said that unless the principals understood the underlying rationale for certain practices, they were more likely to perceive their principal supervisors as directive and evaluative rather than supportive and therefore resist them.

These principal supervisors also reported that modeling required them to actively resist the temptation, and occasional pressure from some principals, to step in and do work for their principals. One principal supervisor, responding to a principal who asked her to run professional development for the principal's teachers, explained, "We can't do it for you. We cannot come in and address your staff. Your staff needs to see *you* as the leader. Your staff needs to see *you* giving the feedback about what they're not doing right. Not us."

As an example of modeling in practice, we observed a principal supervisor working with a principal who was a novice at identifying high-quality instruction. Prior to a classroom visit, the principal supervisor confirmed with the principal that she would be modeling how to observe students working in small groups to understand the rigor of their task and the students' understanding of what they were doing and why. During the classroom visits, the principal supervisor stayed physically close to the principal and narrated what she was seeing in the classroom and the extent to which she thought it fit the standards related to task rigor and understanding—a form of modeling thinking. Just after the observation, the principal reflected on the experience aloud and in writing and planned to practice what he learned before his supervisor's next visit.

Principal supervisors in the positive cases also modeled ways of thinking as instructional leaders. As one explained, such modeling involved "talking through what [the principal's] thinking is and then helping him to see where that might take him, so the principal has time to stop and actually think about why he is making the decisions that he's making . . . [A principal] will oftentimes jump to decision-making without stepping back and really thinking about how he's making [decisions], who he's involving in the process, and then what are the consequences of that."

This principal supervisor described this process with the following example, corroborated by the principal:

> So [a principal] asks staff to do something . . . [saying], "I want you all to make sure that you post objectives [in your classrooms]" . . . and expects [that] once said, that it is going to happen . . . And one of the teachers says, "No, I don't want to do that," or a teacher doesn't do it and then . . . [the principal's] immediate reaction is "Okay, we've got to do something to get this teacher out of here" . . . without understanding . . . the culture of [the] school. [The principal] doesn't necessarily put herself in the position of those she's attempting to move . . . [So my work involved] taking her back to where the initial thought happens so that she can understand there are other options, and why is she thinking that—what about her and her approach to the work is taking her there?

In the negative cases, principal supervisors more often directed principals to engage in various tasks rather than modeling how. As we noted previously, school visits from several of these supervisors typically involved them observing classrooms (with or without the principal) and then sending emails detailing next steps for the principals and teachers.

Some of these principal supervisors expressed a limited understanding of the difference between a teaching and learning approach and a telling one. One described a school visit to his coach: "We were visiting those [math and enrichment classes] to see if they were using the computer-based system . . . I did an observation and started drafting out what those look-fors are. I directed [the principal that] by next week she needed to have an outline of what those look-fors are. I was feeling like I was being in teaching mode on the whole idea." The coach asked, "How? What is the principal learning to do, and what's your role in their learning?" The principal supervisor responded that the look-fors helped him as the supervisor monitor implementation and decide how the principal should proceed.

These principal supervisors also tended to step in and do work on principals' behalf, rather than teach them to lead the work themselves. One principal supervisor referred to a fellow supervisor who took this approach as an "uber-principal." In fact, that principal supervisor told us she did budgeting for principals, for example, rather than helping them learn to use budget decisions to leverage high-quality teaching and learning. She elaborated that when she works with a principal who has instructionally focused budgeting as a growth area, "I go back into their budgets with the fiscal analyst and I find out how much money they've recaptured by having the sub [substitute teacher] in the position that had the full cost of a teacher encumbered, and I recapture it and use it for something else." When asked how, if at all, the principal participated in that process, this principal supervisor responded that some issues were too "high-stakes" to take time to involve the principals.

In another example, a supervisor reported that several principals were not using school-based coaches in effective ways. The supervisor went directly to the coaches and reassigned them to different classrooms, a responsibility formally within the principals' purview. This principal supervisor explained that it was more efficient to just make this change on her own rather than engage the principals in the process.

Talk moves. Talk is central to professional learning as adults engage in dialog with a mentor or colleagues about their target practice, current practice, or how to improve. Some talk moves open up opportunities for ambitious practice changes, while other moves can shut down learning. We found marked differences in how principal supervisors in the positive and negative cases talked with their principals, and these differences were consistent with distinctions in sociocultural learning theory.

In the positive cases, principal supervisors made talk moves that engaged principals in understanding their current practice in ways that created urgency and action toward improvement. In a typical example, one principal supervisor described how, at a school with low student achievement test scores, she consistently saw unambitious teaching in classrooms but high scores on that principal's ratings of teachers in the district teacher evaluation system. This principal supervisor worked with the principal to organize and analyze the test score, observation, and evaluation data and to ask probing questions across the data. As he explained:

> Every one of the teachers got 100 percent on their performance evaluations. They only have about 57 percent of their kids meeting or exceeding the state standards. A third of their kids didn't pass the [state test]. When every one of the teachers got 100 percent on their performance evaluation, I said "Who's 100 percent? You? Who? How does everybody get 100 percent?" [The principal said], "You have forced me to really understand this and take a look at it and really see. I get it." Because what incentive do teachers have to improve if they're already a 95 and they don't get outcomes with kids? Why should they change their behavior?

Another principal supervisor described how he used talk moves to probe for principals' understanding of the quality of teaching in their classrooms and next steps for teachers' and their own growth:

> We go visit a number of classrooms. We come back and talk through it . . . I'll say, "OK, we saw this learning target in this classroom. Let's try to interpret quickly what standards that teacher was teaching to and let's look it up and see if they got it right." Not from a

> perspective of trying to catch them doing it wrong—this is more for my perspective of making sure that the principals aren't just making assumptions and then come and report to me all these great things that they're concluding based on assumptions. That they take the extra step and look for themselves to make sure. And trying to develop that as being a habitual thing.

Several of these principal supervisors also emphasized that such challenging talk was especially important for their principals who are experienced at instructional leadership. One explained that even with those principals there is always room "to probe, sharpen, and explore" how the principal could lead even more powerfully. Another admitted that a couple of his principals had far more experience than he did with instructional leadership. But his principals reported that his questions made them stronger instructional leaders.

By contrast, principal supervisors in the negative cases tended not to engage their principals in talk of this kind. In one case, a principal reported that her principal supervisor would walk into classrooms, "stand at the back, take some notes, walk away, and send me an email a couple of days later and say how horrible the observation was. If it's really that bad, then you should have been compelled to have a conversation with that teacher or at least a conversation with me: 'Hey, this is what I just saw. Let's go into the class together this next period, observe it together, and find out where we can help support this teacher and improve his instruction.'"

Some of the principal supervisors in the negative cases said they were using talk moves as teaching moves in their one-on-one work with principals, but we did not see evidence of their doing so in practice. In other words, these principal supervisors were adopting the talk of using talk moves. While they did in fact often lead with questions, the questions tended to be closed rather than open-ended—asking for simple answers in ways that suggested they were engaging with only limited understanding of how to use talk moves as a teaching strategy and still checking up on principals rather than engaging them in their own learning. Such exchanges also were typically short, with the principal supervisor simply asking the principal what was happening and what the principal was doing about it without further discussion.

For instance, one principal supervisor described his job as "working with principals on becoming stronger instructional leaders." But when asked for an example of how he does that work, he said, "I scheduled weekly meetings with the . . . new elementary principals . . . I go to their buildings and chat . . . and then if they have something, they call me. I try not to bother them." A principal described the visits from this supervisor in terms of his use of superficial talk: "When [my principal supervisor] visits . . . he brings with him typically a message of 'We're in this together,' and 'You're doing a good job,' and 'What can I do to support you?' I think that would sum up most of his visits."

Differentiation. As many of the preceding examples reflect, principal supervisors in the positive cases worked with each of their principals differently in one-on-one settings, depending on each principal's capacity for instructional leadership or their learning plans specifically to support their growth. These principal supervisors typically used concrete evidence of principals' ability to engage in specific aspects of instructional leadership as the basis for this differentiation. As one principal expressed:

> [There are] . . . principals who have less experience than I do. They're in their first year or their second year and I'm, even now with four years, in a different place than where they are. So, I think that they [the principal supervisors] all understand that and I think it directly impacts the way that they work with us. I think that sometimes it's created some confusion in some ways because we're not all necessarily asking for the same thing all the time, so I actually think on their end, it's a rather difficult job to manage. It's pretty analogous to having a class full of heterogeneous students where people need very, very different things.

One principal supervisor said that her efforts to differentiate meant working on a range of areas, depending on principals' learning plans:

> It may be about sitting with their professional development team, listening to what they're trying to put together, and then asking

> questions to help them through that. It could be in terms of looking at classes—an initiative that the school may have and they want to see how the instruction is going, or it could be because they want a different lens on a teacher that they feel is not performing up to par and they just want my input on that. It could be a parent meeting that they're having to explain the data and how to look at the data, or things like strategies like how to read with your children, or building vocabulary—activities that they can do at home. It could be around having conversations with some principals that may be stressed and overwhelmed and talking crazy, like "I'm quitting."

One of these principal supervisors showed us observation notes that he had taken during visits with a middle school principal over the course of the year indicating that the principal could already engage in many instructional leadership activities at a high level. This principal supervisor differentiated his support to this principal's instructional leadership by positioning her as a mentor for other middle school principals. The principal supervisor then gave her feedback on her leadership of other principals. But, when the same principal assumed the leadership of a high school, she struggled to engage in instructional leadership practices in that setting. The principal supervisor observed the principal in her new setting and together they identified that the principal still demonstrated strengths in supporting classroom teachers, but she now needed help working with high school department heads. The two then focused their efforts together on that aspect of her instructional leadership.

Many of these principal supervisors differentiated their supports to principals by building on principals' strengths. For example, one principal supervisor worked with a principal to conduct a comprehensive self-assessment against the district's definition of high-quality principal leadership and identified conducting classroom observations as a strength, but fostering teacher learning teams as an area for growth. The principal supervisor then worked with the principal to adapt his successful methods for observing classrooms to the observation of teacher learning teams as one strategy to help improve his ability to support teacher teams.

The principal supervisors in the negative cases also worked with each principal differently, but often based on their school's student test score results, not their demonstrated capacity to engage in instructional leadership. This strategy led to some mismatches between the support these principal supervisors provided and principals' actual instructional leadership strengths and areas for growth, since student test scores are, at best, a weak proxy for principals' capacity, especially in districts that have committed to staffing their low scoring schools with their strongest principals.

For example, one principal supervisor spent the majority of their time with principals in low-performing, low-growth schools. One of this principal supervisor's principals had been placed in such a school because of her demonstrated ability to improve the quality of teaching in a similar school. During an interview, she reported that "[my principal supervisor] . . . cares about me. I enjoy our conversations. But I really just need to get to work here. I would think their time's better spent elsewhere."

In sum, even though all districts aimed to reinvent their principal supervisor role, in practice principal supervisors did not all understand or execute their role in those new ways when they worked with principals one-on-one. These differences were not subtle. Some principal supervisors frequently and proficiently took a teaching and learning approach to helping principals grow as instructional leaders. This approach included helping principals lead their own learning and using specific moves characteristic of skilled mentors. Others took a more traditional supervisory stance, mainly visiting schools to check up on or direct principals rather than teach them how to continuously grow their instructional leadership. Perhaps not surprisingly, we associated the principal supervisors who took a teaching and learning approach with positive results related to principals' growth as instructional leaders and negative or negligible results with the latter.

CHAPTER 3

Teaching and Learning in Principals Meetings

PRINCIPAL SUPERVISOR NANCY ESCALERA opened the March meeting of her fourteen principals in the library of Kennedy Middle School by displaying a picture of a road heading off into the sunset. She explained:

> Let's start where we do, reminding ourselves where we are in our work together. We decided this year we are going to focus on how we lead our school improvement planning process—to make sure that process is a real driver of equity in our buildings. We started with looking at examples of the kinds of leadership we wanted to see in ourselves. Then, we have been working through our plan for the year, starting with how we are building strong teacher teams throughout the school to serve as our foundation. Today, we are looking at how we observe those teams to provide them with regular feedback on how well they are working together on their own learning plans. We are moving toward spring sessions on how we look at the data we have been collecting to figure out our staffing and professional development plans for next year.

She then prompted the principals to turn and talk with a colleague about their personal goals for the session and how they would participate that day to advance their learning. When she invited the principals to briefly share with the whole group, one said, "I appreciate how Reggie always has his learning plan out in front of him every session in OneNote and he's taking notes right there so all his session notes are in one place so he can reflect on them later." Another said, "Yeah, Sumara showed me how this is an area of growth for her—the observation part—and how she built this visit into her learning plan. She also has a note to figure out how to follow up so it's not a one-time thing."

Principal Supervisor Escalera then turned the meeting over to the host principal to frame the first activity, an extended observation of teacher teams. She explained that the host principal had made strengthening teacher teams an area of focus for several years and that they were there to see teams working at a relatively high level and to help the principal think more deeply about the systems the teacher teams were using to monitor their own progress. The host principal then provided brief background on the evolution of teacher teams at her school and reviewed the current process for monitoring their progress.

The principals spent the next sixty minutes observing two teacher teams that regularly met that morning. In the team meetings, teachers shared examples of student work and calibrated their assessments—discussing how each piece of work reflected elements of the science standards they were focused on that week. Principal Supervisor Escalera sat with her two new principals in the back of the room where they could discuss what they were seeing in real time and observe both the teachers and other principals.

When the principals reconvened, they worked in small groups to compare what they saw. Principal Supervisor Escalera then opened the whole-group discussion: "Let's start with coming together around the basic 'what.' What did we see, in low-inference terms? Just describe it." Escalera charted the responses, occasionally asking other principals to engage critically, with questions like, "How does that compare with what you saw, Reggie?" and, "Sumara might say there is judgment in that description; how might you word it to take the judgment out so our judgments later aren't skewed when you look at all the data you have?"

Escalera then shifted the conversation with, "Now, how have teachers been self-assessing? Let's get that up and talk about if we saw anything today that might relate to those results." Principals then looked at a sample of data that the teacher teams had been using to track their progress. In their discussion, the principals identified that the first group of teachers seemed to be viewing their work as involving strong calibration and identification of next steps for individual teachers consistent with the grade-level standards. The principals reflected together that their own observations supported the teachers' assessments.

The second group of teachers provided data on their meetings that mainly indicated that they enjoyed getting together. But the teachers provided little evidence that during meetings they had actually been critically reflecting on the quality of their own practice and working together to improve. The visiting principals' observations showed that on that day these teachers mainly shared examples of student work and how each saw the sample as relating to standards. The teachers engaged in little discussion or calibration across the team about what counted as evidence of the standards and how the team might move forward together.

The visiting principals then divided into smaller groups to prepare feedback for the host principal. Afterward, the principals worked individually and in pairs to reflect on the implications of the school visit for their next steps at their own schools.

Principal Supervisor Escalera concluded the meeting by reminding the principals that she had put some information items and due dates in their shared online calendar. She said, "Do what you do to take care of that stuff so we can keep focused on our work together."

Later, Principal Supervisor Escalera reflected on the meeting:

> What you just saw was us totally flipping the old script. When I was a principal, these meetings were with all principals in the district office. They were one presentation after another. Sometimes it would maybe be about the new math curriculum. We would talk about it once and then move on to the next thing. Now, I work with my principals to make the meetings about them and their learning. At the start of the year, we talk about their learning goals and plans and how

> the meetings can support those plans. Then, we organize it like a curriculum. Not a list of topics, but month-to-month building on what we have been doing and deepening the learning. Like, in September, we couldn't have done this—observe a meeting and compare it to other data. That was too much. So we analyzed one piece of data together first. Then, we worked on observing to describe what we see before we evaluate. And now what you saw was us bringing it together. And they love it. They love being in each other's schools. And they really own it. I was out last month and they decided they didn't want to reschedule and they just ran the plan themselves. That's leadership.

Across our study sites, principals' engagement in meetings such as this one facilitated by Principal Supervisor Escalera was high. Principals consistently arrived to the meetings on time, with their "homework" completed, and actively participated in small- and large-group meeting activities. During these meetings, principals also engaged in progressively more challenging instructional leadership activities over time, as illustrated in the preceding vignette.

These principals tended to report that they valued these meetings specifically as supports for their growth as instructional leaders. For example, one principal reported that the meetings "are very much like a professional learning community. We get input around different pedagogical issues, different administrative issues. We talk about them. We look at our data . . . So, a big part of what we do in those meetings is around school improvement." Similarly, a principal from a smaller district described their meetings as a forum where "we're talking about how do you lead those types of [teaching and learning] changes, rather than how do you lead organizational-type change or managerial types of changes."

As in the previous chapter, we call the principal supervisors we associated with such results the positive cases. We do so here not only because of the positive results related to these supervisors' leadership of principals meetings but also for consistency with chapter 2, because the meetings associated with such results were convened by the same principal supervisors who appeared in the positive cases of one-on-one work with principals.

By contrast, the principal supervisors we associated with negative outcomes in their one-on-one work with principals also tended to demonstrate negative results in their principals meetings, including principals' low attendance and frequent late arrivals, early departures, and incomplete homework. Principals typically reported that the meetings did not support their growth as instructional leaders and many openly complained that they were not useful. As one principal reported, "It's drudgery . . . It should not be that I dread it." During one small-group activity in a meeting we observed, a principal said to her colleagues, "You guys, this is really a joke," sparking a prolonged conversation in the small group about matters unrelated to the target task of working to develop a professional development plan for the next school year. A principal in a smaller district where all the principals met together said that those meetings were "85 percent management and 15 percent instructional." When these principals did talk about enjoying their principals meetings, they mainly appreciated the time to consult with their principal colleagues.

To what extent did the principal supervisors in the positive and negative cases differ in how they led their principals meetings, and how might that also account for principals' starkly different experiences with their supervisors?

COMMUNITIES OF PRACTICE VERSUS TRADITIONAL PRINCIPALS MEETINGS

Our conceptual framework called our attention to two broad differences in principal supervisors' leadership of their regular principals meetings. Namely, the principal supervisors in the positive cases:

- intentionally organized their principals meetings around progressively more challenging authentic instructional leadership tasks, instead of, for example, largely administrative matters; and

- facilitated the meetings using specific teaching and learning moves, rather than practices that foster task completion and compliance in ways that can interfere with professional growth.

In this chapter, we detail these differences.

Authentic Tasks in a Scope and Sequence

Visit a principals meeting of one of the principal supervisors in the positive cases, and you typically would see the principals working together on authentic instructional leadership activities in real time at a school site. For example, one such meeting took place at a member principal's school and focused on helping principals deepen their ability to help their teachers improve their core instruction, in this case, for students eligible for services for English language learners (whom the host principal called "ELLs" and others refer to as "emergent bilingual students"). At previous meetings, the principals had worked on basic observation skills related to what counts as evidence of quality teaching, how to talk with students to check for their understanding of classroom activities, and strategies for note taking. At this meeting, principals were taking the next step in their development: learning how to observe classrooms with particular attention to the experiences of students learning English as an additional language.

The host principal opened the meeting by sharing her own background as a student who first arrived in the district thirty years ago from a Spanish-speaking country. She then described her approach to working with teachers on specific teaching practices she considered high leverage for helping ELLs. She explained that she hires only teachers with a special credential related to teaching ELLs, but that those teachers still come with gaps in their skills and she also wants her teachers to have access to the latest, research-based practices. She shared with the principals a protocol she developed with her teachers to guide classroom observations with a specific focus on the experiences of those students. She asked her fellow principals to use the guide for conducting their own observations of three particular teachers and plan to give her feedback on what they saw and how to improve the protocol. The principals spent ninety minutes observing the three classrooms, debriefing what they saw, and providing the host principal with feedback. The principal supervisor then led a conversation with the whole group about implications of the experience for their own work to support students in similar situations at their schools.

When principal supervisors in the positive cases convened their principals at other locations, such as the district's central office or another meeting facility, they still engaged principals in authentic instructional leadership tasks. For instance, one principal supervisor supported his principals' leadership of school improvement planning by periodically convening his principals at the central office to discuss data about their progress toward their school improvement goals with progressively more varied data across the year.

In one such meeting, principals posted displays of one of their goals, their professional development plans for teachers related to that goal, and data about implementation of those plans and any results for teaching practice and student learning. All of the principals circulated to each display and wrote comments and questions for each principal to consider. The principal supervisor then paired the principals to synthesize the input and plan next steps. The principal supervisor concluded the meeting by saying that the group had up to fifteen minutes for compliance-related topics and other announcements, briefly reminded the principals about upcoming events, and invited principals to share information with each other.

While difficult to see in the single meeting examples, many principal supervisors in the positive cases intentionally planned out their meetings for the year as a *scope and sequence*—an integrated set of experiences that aimed to engage principals in progressively more challenging instructional leadership tasks over time. For instance, the principal supervisor intentionally scheduled the meeting at the school site focused on ELLs after doing substantial work with her principals on how to conduct classroom observations together and the importance of using data about student talk to understand the quality of teaching.

The meeting on school improvement planning was the last in a series in which the principal supervisor had principals work with feedback and progressively better school data over time to monitor their progress. That principal supervisor showed us a calendar of all her meetings over the course of the year and described how she ordered the meetings in a learning sequence. She explained that the meetings would address various topics but the main theme for the entire year was principals' leadership of school improvement planning processes. She then organized the meetings to take place at specific schools depending on the content of the meeting. She explained that the first meeting was at a school that was fairly far along in developing systems to support continuous school improvement, in order to help principals see a relatively fully executed approach to serve as a model. The next meetings focused on helping principals ensure that they had the right teacher teams in place to support continuous improvement and on working with one or two data points. Later meetings focused on helping principals build the capacity of those teams in working with increasingly complex data.

Meetings convened by principal supervisors in the positive cases stood in sharp contrast to those of the principal supervisors in the negative cases, which proceeded more like traditional administrative meetings—focused on compliance or operational matters, not authentic leadership tasks, and organized meeting-to-meeting, without a logical progression, let alone one related to principals' growth as instructional leaders. For instance, one principal supervisor held two meetings in a computer lab and prompted principals to work with staff from the Accountability and Budget offices to complete end-of-year paperwork. At another meeting, a principal supervisor rotated his principals through a series of presentations by central office staff about various new resources and requirements from the central office. When we asked one principal about her experience in the meeting, she said, "These meetings are just the same [as in the past], only smaller." According to another principal, "If I have a question, I just ask someone. I don't need a meeting."

In other cases, the principal supervisors seemed to conflate focusing on principals' instructional leadership with focusing on instruction more broadly. For instance, one principal supervisor turned one of her meetings over to a university-based teacher educator who engaged principals in a professional development workshop typically provided to teachers on ambitious science instruction. The principal supervisor then asked the principals to derive implications for their own leadership—the only nod to the principals' practice during that meeting. Principals generally reported that such sessions sharpened their ability to see high-quality instruction, but admitted that they were not always sure what the implications were for how they, in turn, supported teachers.

Facilitation as Teaching and Learning

As they facilitated the meetings, the principal supervisors in the positive cases took a teaching and learning approach consistent with our conceptual framework. As in their one-on-one work with principals, this approach included joint work moves, modeling, challenging talk, differentiation, and brokering, with some differences related to principal supervisors' use of those moves in a meeting setting compared to when principal supervisors worked with their principals one-on-one. For instance, in chapter 2, we discussed how principal supervisors engaged in brokering in their one-on-one work mainly by bridging or connecting principals to their colleagues and other resources for their learning. The brokering in principals meetings included bridging as well as *buffering*, or protecting, principals from interruptions to their focus on instructional leadership. In addition, in the meetings, principal supervisors in the positive cases positioned each principal as a learning resource for the group in ways socio-cultural learning theory highlights as important to the development of expertise.

Joint work moves. As the preceding examples reflect, principal supervisors in the positive cases routinely emphasized the value of principals' growth as instructional leaders by focusing the vast majority of their meetings not just on instructional matters but on principals' instructional leadership specifically. These principal supervisors also underscored for their principals that the meetings were settings for their *mutual* learning. As one principal supervisor explained, "It's a professional learning community model that you [principals and their supervisors] learn together and we help each other, and we look at student learning results together, and we try to improve our practice together and share best practices."

For example, one principal supervisor opened a meeting with his principals by sharing that not only were the principals building their knowledge of the district's new instructional framework defining high-quality teaching, but he was as well. He said he organized the meeting with principals' learning as the main focus but also to help him "learn along the way as well, because I want to get better at what *I'm* doing." He then introduced a coach who led the group through a series of activities related to understanding one of the framework elements. Throughout the meeting, the principal supervisor asked questions as a learner such as, "Does engagement look different for boys and girls? I'm asking because we have very uneven enrollment in advanced science and math in secondary. I'm asking, What can I do to support my principals in turning that around?" Such a participation strategy may have been an especially powerful way to reinforce the value of growing as instructional leaders when, as in this example, the principal supervisor was also the district superintendent.

In another example of reinforcing mutual learning, a principal supervisor opened several of her meetings with a discussion of her own professional learning targets and the feedback her principals had provided to her up to that point. She asked that as the principals moved through the meeting, they pay attention to how well her leadership incorporated their feedback. At the end of each meeting, she distributed an "exit ticket" that asked principals for additional feedback and again reflected with them on that feedback at a subsequent meeting.

Several principal supervisors in the positive cases also used their meetings to reinforce the value of principals' growth as instructional leaders by designing the content of their meetings specifically to reinforce the instructional leadership focus of their one-on-one work with principals. As one principal supervisor described:

> So the stuff we do in . . . meetings supports the work we do individually. When I'm at the site I may go with the principal to see their

> focus teacher, ask them what they're doing with their focus teacher. Then in our meetings, they get in . . . groups and they actually share feedback they've given to a focus teacher with their [group] to get feedback. They may share a success story they've had with the focus teacher. Or in our last meeting on Thursday, the focus teacher was one way to look at the data to see if the impact of their leadership with that focus teacher actually impacted the student-level data.

Another principal supervisor reviewed her principals' individual learning plans and identified principal leadership around mathematics instruction as a common growth area for her principals. She then worked with a math coach to plan out a series of principals meetings to address principals' specific learning plan goals related to mathematics instruction. The principal supervisor then circled back to her principals in their one-on-one meetings and asked them, what adjustments, if any, they would make in their plans to lead their own learning now that they know how the principals' meetings would support their leadership in mathematics.

Principal supervisors in the positive cases also jointly organized the meetings with their principals. For instance, one collaborated with a rotating committee of principals on setting meeting agendas and cofacilitation. And as the vignette that opens this chapter illustrates, many of these principal supervisors partnered with a different principal each month to host a visit at his or her school that the two cofacilitated.

By contrast, principal supervisors in the negative cases made decisions about their meetings that did not reinforce the value of principals' growth as instructional leaders or even, in some cases, had the opposite effect. For example, two principal supervisors facilitated meetings early in the year on helping principals work well with data to understand and address teaching quality. By winter, agenda items began to focus on operational matters and the principal supervisors used their last two meetings for principals to complete end-of-year paperwork.

Two other principal supervisors turned a series of meetings over to outside consultants who addressed how to help teachers set performance goals. The principal supervisors spent long stretches of time outside the meetings on the phone or at other locations. When their principals provided feedback to the supervisors that the consultants were not effective, the principal supervisors told them that they would be working with the consultants all year regardless.

Modeling. In principals meetings, principal supervisors in the positive cases also frequently modeled for principals how to think and act as instructional leaders. The following example illustrates how modeling even in single meetings involved not just one move but many metacognitive comments, demonstrations, and opportunities to reflect and practice.

The meeting took place at a high school and focused on helping principals use data about student talk in classrooms to determine if students were deepening their understanding of particular concepts. The principal supervisor framed the activity with metacognitive comments about why capturing data about student talk provided important evidence of the quality of classroom instruction. She engaged the principals in a brief discussion of strategies for capturing student talk, most of which involved sitting with students in particular ways.

As the classroom visits began, a group of five principals entered one English class where students were working in small groups to discuss a common text. The principals stood at the perimeter of the room where the closest student group was hard to hear, and otherwise did not use the strategies they had just identified. When the principal supervisor arrived, first she stood back with the principals for a few moments and made various metacognitive comments about how standing so far away made it too difficult to hear student talk. She asked questions aloud, rhetorically and modeling thinking, such as, "Which student group will I sit with first and why would that one be good to start with?" and "Which strategy that we discussed for joining a group might make sense now?"

After a brief pause, she walked directly to a table of students and called her principals closer to observe. When the students stopped talking and looked up at her, the principal supervisor briefly introduced herself to the students, said she was just there to learn more about what they were working on in tenth-grade English, and asked whether they would mind if she sat in. The students agreed and the supervisor then knelt down close to the group and asked a few brief questions, such as, "What are you working on now?" and "Why this activity—how does it help you with what you are working on?" The principal supervisor then remained with that group for several minutes before getting up and jotting down some notes.

After repeating that process with another group of students, the principal supervisor convened the five principals in the hall for a quick debrief. She asked the principals to recount how she conducted herself in the classroom and the pros and cons of her choices. After taking a few minutes to plan their approach, the principals visited the next classroom, with the principal supervisor taking notes on the principals' efforts for later discussion.

In another example, a principal supervisor opened a meeting about principal leadership of school improvement planning by having a "fishbowl" conversation with one principal. First, she said they all knew that school teams often add so many goals and strategies to their plans that the plans become hard to use. Through this fishbowl conversation, she would demonstrate how they could work together to practice leading their school teams to create sharper areas of focus using a particular questioning strategy. That strategy involved interrogating their rationales for particular choices and prioritizing those areas of focus that rested on relatively strong rationales. Such a strategy could also help schools that already have a manageable number of focus areas to reaffirm those choices and their shared understanding of why to proceed with them. The principal supervisor asked the principals to take notes on the conversation that they could subsequently use for discussion and to determine their next steps.

She then interviewed the principal about his school's rationale for certain elements in his school improvement plan, modeling particular questioning strategies. Afterward, the principals discussed which of those questioning strategies seemed especially useful for pushing the principal's thinking and how they might use similar questioning with one another and later with the teacher teams back at their schools. Principals then got into pairs and practiced those questioning strategies.

Principal supervisors in the negative cases, by contrast, generally did not work alongside their principals in the ways that modeling demands. More often, they directed or told principals to engage in particular activities rather than modeled or demonstrated how to do so.

For example, for one meeting, principals brought several teachers from their schools to work with them on an activity that required them to display the main goals and strategies of their school improvement plans, post written comments on the other schools' plans, and then reconvene to discuss the comments they received. Several teams had not prepared their displays in advance, as the principal supervisor had instructed, so the principal supervisor told all the groups to take twenty minutes to do so. During this time, the teams that had completed their homework mostly engaged in informal conversation while they waited for the meeting to start.

Then, during the discussion period, the principal supervisor circulated around the room and interrupted individual teams to tell them what changes to make in their plans. For instance, at one point she told a group to "broaden the statement" about their instructional focus so that it applied to all teachers in their school, even though the school team had designed the statement intentionally to target particular teachers the principal saw as leverage points for overall school improvement. The principal supervisor told another group to make sure one of their focus areas addressed their school's low scores on the state mathematics achievement test.

Similarly, at another meeting, a small group of principals was grappling with the pros and cons of different approaches to improving instructional rigor at one school. Their principal supervisor walked by the group, overheard part of the discussion, and interrupted the debate with specific instructions that the principal should focus on using best practices to support reading comprehension.

Talk moves. Principal supervisors in the positive cases also frequently used talk moves in principals meetings to deepen principals' understanding of what instructional leadership involves and how and why to engage in it. The positive examples of modeling just described also featured the use of talk in the form of metacognitive statements and discussion strategies to foster learning. Other talk moves pushed principals to get much more precise in their thinking about their observations and use of evidence. The following example illustrates both.

After one series of classroom observations at a principals meeting, a principal supervisor started the whole-group discussion by asking principals what they saw related to the focus of that particular observation, student engagement. Principals initially responded with general comments about the classroom, such as "There's too much stuff on the board." One principal said that he thought the objective of the lesson was unclear because he had asked some of the students what it was and they didn't know. The principal supervisor challenged the principals to sharpen their answers, prompting them with such comments and questions as, "What difference does it make how much stuff is on the board to how the teacher is actually teaching?", "Maybe the students do know what the objective is, but you asked them in a way that was confusing to them," and "How do each of your ideas provide an indication of the quality of student engagement specifically?"

The principal supervisor then asked if principals saw any evidence related to particular grade-level standards. The principals all replied quickly that they did not. The principal supervisor asked, "What's your evidence?" and pressed the principals to "show me" and "convince me" that those teachers may not be teaching to the standards. Several principals reported that they saw standards written on the board in one classroom. The principal supervisor challenged these principals further, asking if they saw specific evidence that the standards on the board related to what the teacher was actually doing. The principals acknowledged that they did not. Several principals pointed out that when they asked students what they were working on, the students provided different answers, with one group indicating that they didn't know. The principal supervisor then asked the principals to continue the discussion by talking in pairs and to bring back to the whole group their consensus on at least one claim about the quality of teaching in one classroom, with multiple forms of supporting evidence.

As this example illustrates, principal supervisors in the positive cases also used the group setting of principals meetings to foster challenging talk *among* their principals. In another instance, a principal supervisor was framing an activity in which principals would provide one another with feedback on their progress in three areas since the previous year. He said that the one ground rule for the presenting principals was that they "were not allowed to talk about anything that they did not have evidence to support that they did it." The principals giving feedback had to make sure they prompted the presenters to provide deeper evidence from their principal colleagues.

By contrast, principal supervisors in the negative cases often used directive talk moves, which typically foster compliance rather than learning. We provided several examples of such directive talk in the modeling discussion, for instance, where the principal supervisor told principals what changes to make in their school improvement plans without exploring with the principals why they might make those changes or talking through how the principals might figure out the changes for themselves.

Principal supervisors in the negative cases also fostered shallow talk—discussions that only superficially engaged principals and did not prompt them to examine their practice in ways that supported their growth as instructional leaders. For instance, in one meeting, the principal supervisor instructed principals to observe several classrooms and then asked them to share "wows," or positive comments, and "wonders," or areas the principal may want to consider improving. Principals listed each in "popcorn" fashion with brief responses like "Hopeful," "Nice vibe," "Paying attention," "No distractions," "Great celebration of student work," and "The hallways look great." Several comments from principals related to how the teachers were, in the words of one, "really connecting with the kids." The principal supervisor then shifted to the next item on the agenda without any follow-up or concluding comments.

In another example, one principal supervisor started a principals meeting by speaking for more than fifteen minutes straight about principals' important role in supporting the superintendent's initiatives around improving instruction and closing achievement gaps. Following this introduction, he instructed the principals to observe classrooms to see if they were witnessing "gap-closing instruction." The supervisor did not define such instruction, instead simply asking principals for "look-fors"—what they would expect to see in the classrooms if the teachers were demonstrating gap-closing instruction. Principals brainstormed different general observation points, such as "student talk" and "tasks," without specifying what about the talk and tasks would make for gap-closing instruction. The supervisor listed those ideas on chart paper and then instructed principals to visit particular classrooms and come back together for a whole-group discussion.

During the observations, none of the principals took notes on the look-fors, possibly because the look-fors were available only on the chart paper in the main meeting room, and only a couple of the principals we shadowed took any notes at all during their observations. Back in the whole group, the principal supervisor asked for comments from the principals on what they saw, but did not comment himself, other than to call on the next speaker. After about fifteen minutes, the supervisor said, "Okay, let's stop for a break. Be back in fifteen minutes." When the principals returned, the supervisor turned the meeting over to a presentation by another central office staff person who explained upcoming changes in high school graduation requirements.

Brokering. As we elaborate in our conceptual framework, brokering is especially important to learning in groups. The bridging aspect of brokering helps ensure that the resources available to support the group's learning are not limited to those already available within the group. Buffering provides the group with protection from outside interference with their learning.

Principal supervisors in the positive cases typically bridged or brought other people in to their principals meetings to enhance their efforts to support principals' growth as instructional leaders. As an example, a principal supervisor had a math coach from the central office attend a series of principals meetings to help principals understand the implications of the new math curriculum for their instructional leadership practice. The principal supervisor explained that even though she herself was fairly familiar with the new curriculum, the coach brought important expertise into the group.

Examples in the positive cases stood out for *how* the principal supervisor brought in outside resources: in nearly all the cases, consistent with the idea of brokering as translating highlighted in our conceptual framework, the principal supervisor actively worked with the outside guests to ensure that their participation proceeded from a teaching and learning stance or otherwise promised to support principals' growth as instructional leaders. For instance, in the math coach example, the principal supervisor described the coach as a ready resource for her group of principals because the coach already knew how to take a teaching and learning approach. Still, she met with the coach to review and provide feedback on the coach's lesson plan for each meeting.

And in fact, during meetings, we observed firsthand this coach taking a teaching and learning approach. In one session at a school, she demonstrated modeling and talk moves while facilitating the whole-group discussion after a series of classroom observations framed by the host principal. The coach began by asking principals to talk in pairs about the extent to which they saw the teachers teaching math in ways that reflected a distinction the principals were learning to make between learning procedures and learning with conceptual understanding. She then shared her notes from her own observations as a common model or jumping-off point for discussion. She framed the notes by saying that when she entered one classroom, the students "had two points, and they were going through the point slope formula to determine the equation of the straight line. They were doing this over and over again. So I spoke individually with three students . . . I'm quite certain that those students did not know that what they had created was the equation to come up with the line to connect the two points." The coach went on to say that even though the teacher had set up an activity that prompted students to construct the slope formula for themselves rather than just memorize it, the students were still not demonstrating an understanding of what they were doing. So, she explained, if the principals just looked at the task the teacher set out as evidence of teaching quality, they would misinterpret what was actually happening for students. The group then discussed the other evidence from the observations and next steps for the host principal.

When outside guests were not as experienced as this math coach with taking a teaching and learning approach, principal supervisors in the positive cases worked with them more intensively to do so. For instance, two central office staff asked a principal supervisor if they could attend a principals meeting to discuss the district's new writing assessments. The principal supervisor told them that if they wanted to deliver information to principals, they should put that information in writing for her to distribute. Otherwise, they had to work with her in advance of their attending to connect the session to the principals' ongoing learning plan for the meetings and to facilitate the meeting to support principals' learning. The principal supervisor then met with them over several hours to work out their lesson plan.

At the resulting principals meeting, during which the two central office staff presented, they began their segment by sharing learning goals—what they designed the session to help principals know and be able to do—and how the session fit in with the scope and sequence for the meetings. Then, they asked the principals to orient themselves to the work ahead by reviewing the new writing assessment rubric, reflecting on where they thought their school fell on the rubric, and jotting down some evidence they would explore throughout the session to check and improve their ratings. The central office staff then shared brief highlights of how the assessments reflected the new state standards. After they made each point, they gave the principals small- and large-group opportunities to talk through what they were hearing and compare the new assessments to current practice at their school.

This principal supervisor also actively mediated the participation of the central office staff by making metacognitive statements at key points to help principals further connect what they were hearing with their own leadership practice. For example, at one point she clarified that the rubric was not just a tool for their teachers to use for individual student assessments, but one intended to help principals in their professional development of teachers. The principal supervisor also personally facilitated the last twenty minutes of the session, focused on the implications of the new writing assessments for their instructional leadership.

Principal supervisors in the positive cases also buffered, or actively shielded, their principals meetings from interruptions to their instructional leadership focus, including requests from their central office colleagues to present information to principals, or from principals to use meeting time for matters other than their instructional leadership. One principal supervisor explained the importance of buffering by saying, "I think that the core job description of being an instructional leader to the principals has to be protected and it has to be respected . . . It takes fighting our bosses sometimes." This principal supervisor went on to describe how his own supervisor had encouraged him to use an outside consultant to facilitate many of his principals meetings. But this principal supervisor disagreed and actively worked to keep the consultant out of his meetings:

> First of all, I already knew the principals didn't like it [the work the consultant was doing elsewhere in the district]. But then the second thing is that I met the leadership of [the consulting group] and I thought, "Oh, there's no way I can put my principals in front of these guys. Well, so we [another principal supervisor and I] fought it. We fought it furiously. Luckily, we were united and they [the central office leadership] backed off . . . I'm absolutely determined not to turn over my [principals' meetings] and sit back. I just won't do that.

When we asked another principal supervisor why she thought her colleagues had displaced their instructional leadership focus so principals could complete budget paperwork, she sighed. She explained that her principals too sometimes pushed back on her, especially in the spring with so many reports and other things to do. She said when she was principal, she also felt the pressure and sometimes wanted to skip a learning session for herself or her teachers. But, she argued, that is exactly when they need you to stay the course. She said, "We are always too busy and can never be too busy to focus on our most important work" of continuously improving students' classroom experiences.

Principal supervisors in the positive cases also buffered their meetings by limiting any matters not related to principals' growth as instructional leaders to a small fraction of their meeting time. As one described:

> So what I did to buffer is, every month we have two meetings, right, and one is professional development and one is coordinating or compliance-type issues. What I did last year is, I took the second one, which was compliance coordination, out and I said, "We're doing two professional development sessions and no coordination." So, they get the information because most of the stuff you get are things that you can read, and my principals, really, quite honestly, are never going to get a skylight in their schools, so they don't need to hear [the gas and electric company] talk about how that makes the school better. So I just tell everybody, "No, you're not coming." So last year I would not allow anyone into the meetings. I just kept them away, and if there was something that was absolutely essential they got it the last thirty minutes of the second . . . meeting. But most of it's not that essential, to be quite honest.

Another principal supervisor said that he "worked hard" to keep informational and compliance issues to a short period at the end of each meeting. Otherwise, as this principal supervisor explained, they "take on a life of their own and take over the meetings. You would be surprised how many people don't show up for their allotted time. Imagine if we gave them more of the agenda and they didn't show up."

Another said that "for the compliance stuff, I put 90 plus percent of those expectations in writing. At the end of all my meeting agendas I have 'Here are upcoming key dates—pay attention—here are some really important reminders,' and I don't spend any time [on them]. I just in the beginning said [to my principals], 'Don't make my conversation be about compliance or operational stuff. Take care of this stuff.'"

Principal supervisors in the negative cases also brought in, or bridged, outside people as resources but typically did not actively engage with them to ensure they took a teaching and learning stance. These examples also appear to represent ineffective buffering because they involved letting resources into their meetings that took meeting time away from helping principals grow as instructional leaders.

For instance, remember the two central office staff members who wanted time at the principals' meetings to share information about the writing assessments and how one principal supervisor had curated their participation so it proceeded from a teaching and learning approach? We observed those same central office staff members attend meetings of two other principal supervisors without any advance preparation. At the meetings, they delivered a thirty-minute, lecture-style presentation on new writing assessment procedures, allowed a few minutes for questions, and then exited as the principal supervisor transitioned to the next information item on the agenda.

In general, the principals in the negative cases did not decline requests from other central office staff to attend principals meetings to deliver information about various operational and administrative matters. One meeting agenda included eight different topics over a three-hour period. The first segment, only forty-five minutes, involved classroom observations. For the other two hours, principals sat in the host school's library while central office staff reviewed information with them on such topics as new purchasing processes and the Employee Assistance Program.

In another example, as mentioned earlier in the discussion of joint work moves, two principal supervisors in the negative cases also turned about a year's worth of principals meetings over to two outside consultants. Despite feedback from their principals that the coaches were not helpful to their growth as instructional leaders, the principal supervisors continued with the consultants and, for their part, frequently disengaged from meetings by sitting in the back during sessions or leaving for significant stretches of time.

Identifying all group members as learning resources. Mentors facilitate learning in groups by positioning each learner, however novice, as a learning resource for the other members. In so doing, mentors help learners identify as on a trajectory toward mastery, important to their actual progress, and foster collective responsibility for each member's success.

Principal supervisors in the positive cases, in fact, made moves during their principals meetings to identify each principal as a learning resource for the group. As one principal supervisor explained, "[O]ftentimes I'll say to [one of my principals], 'Make sure you sit down next to [another principal] and talk to her about how she set up her last PD [professional development for teachers] because you could really learn a lot about bang, bang, bang or whatever it is.' You know what I mean? They learn so much more from each other than they do from me."

Similarly, at one meeting, a principal asked his principal supervisor what level of detail to include when developing meaningful instructional goals. Instead of giving a specific answer, the principal supervisor called on another principal, whom he knew had been working on the same issue, and asked the two principals to share strategies with each other.

In another instance, the principal supervisor had observed during a district leadership team meeting that one of his principals was already quite skilled at using the district's new definition of high-quality teaching to lead teacher learning at her school site. The principal supervisor subsequently arranged for that principal to lead the upcoming principals' meeting on the use of such frameworks to anchor the design and implementation of teacher professional development.

Earlier in this chapter, we discussed how principal supervisors in the positive cases frequently held their meetings at rotating school sites in an effort to ground their meetings in authentic instructional leadership work in real time. Those examples also reflect their efforts to identify each principal as a learning resource for the others, since these principal supervisors typically focused each visit on an area of strength for the host principal, positioned the host as a main leader of group learning, and rotated the principals meeting through every school in the group to reinforce that every principal member had something to contribute.

To further illustrate, during one meeting, a principal supervisor was observing several classrooms with a subgroup of his principals. Outside one of the classrooms, the principals discussed how the host principal, a fifteen-year veteran in that role, was clearly struggling to work with his teachers on the quality of their classroom instruction. They shared examples of extremely low-quality instruction they saw in the classrooms and wondered if the principal was capable of leading for better instruction. One asked the others if they should even be observing at that principal's school.

The principal supervisor validated their observations, complimenting them on their use of evidence to support their claims. The principal supervisor also shared that this principal has strengths as an instructional leader, particularly in the area of knowing his students. The principal supervisor elaborated, "A student came in one morning to [the principal's] office and the first thing he said was, 'Good morning. Are you hungry?'" The principal supervisor went on to explain that in this instance and in other ways the principal demonstrated the importance of understanding the out-of-school conditions his students faced and addressing them as part of his instructional leadership. The principal supervisor said, "That's the level that he knows his kids" and explained that good instructional leaders continuously seek to understand root causes of each student's school performance, even those outside the classroom.

By contrast, the principal supervisors in the negative cases tended to feature the same few principals as overall instructional leadership experts from whom the others could learn, and typically did not identify the other principals as learning resources. For instance, across nine meetings one principal supervisor routinely called upon the same principal to demonstrate various instructional leadership activities, even when, judging from our own observations of their work, other principals seemed capable of providing a demonstration. Some of these principal supervisors put their principals into "critical friends" groups at the beginning of the year and kept principals in the same groups for the whole year across tasks. Such a strategy is not consistent with creating opportunities for principals to assist one another, because those critical friends groups did not change depending on the issue at hand or principals' developing expertise. Instructions to the critical friends groups, in one example, "to chat and work together" did not reinforce the pairs as an explicit opportunity for principals to assist one another's learning.

Differentiation. Principal supervisors in the positive cases also differentiated opportunities for principals within the meetings based on their own strengths and areas for growth. As they did in one-on-one settings, these principal supervisors differentiated principals' experiences based on evidence of their instructional leadership, not the test scores of the students in their schools.

For instance, earlier we discussed how the principal supervisors in the positive cases typically rotated the school sites at which they convened their meetings, to reflect engagement in authentic tasks and identify each principal as a learning resource for the group. These examples also reflect differentiation in that they involve the principal supervisors creating extended opportunities each year to work with each principal on developing and executing a school visit that emphasizes and aims to extend that host principal's strengths.

In our previous discussion of modeling, we shared an example of how the principal supervisor conducted a fishbowl conversation with a principal to demonstrate how the principals could support one another in focusing their school improvement plans. The principal supervisor also differentiated by tailoring her instructions to the principals based on the degree to which the principals' plans were already focused—to help principals establish or deepen their priorities, depending on their starting points.

In another example, we arrived early to one meeting to find the principal supervisor organizing the seating in her home base for the day, a multipurpose classroom in a member principal's school. When we asked her what she was doing, she explained that she had a good idea about which principals would work well together for the opening activity and she wanted to set up the room so they could begin right away with the principals in the right groups. She showed us how she organized the questions on the protocol in order of progressive difficulty, explaining that this enabled principals to move at their own pace and get as far as made sense for them. She emphasized, "It's just like setting up a classroom."

And the principal supervisors in the negative cases? At this point we have provided various examples of how their meetings mostly focused on operational or compliance matters or engaged principals superficially in instructional topics. But these principal supervisors typically did not differentiate even the operationally focused meetings for their principals. As one experienced principal shared, she understands that the meetings with the Budget and Accountability staff are helpful for new principals, but as a veteran, she already has systems in place to complete such compliance matters. As she put it, "A continual gripe for me is that there is a whole lot of stuff that doesn't pertain to me and I have to sit through meetings and listen to it."

In sum, if you were a principal working with Nancy Escalera or her like-minded principal supervisor colleagues, you had a distinctly different experience in your principals meetings than some of your fellow principals. Your principal supervisor focused your meetings on authentic instructional leadership tasks in real time and organized them in a scope and sequence to support your learning. Your principal supervisor also took a teaching and learning approach to facilitation—for example, using moves such as modeling and brokering to advance your growth as an instructional leader. Even in that group setting, you experienced tasks and roles differentiated or tailored to your particular strengths and areas for growth.

If you were working with a principal supervisor in one of the negative cases, however, chances are you experienced very little difference in the new principals meetings from how your district had previously convened principals. Most meetings focused on the delivery of various kinds of operational or compliance information. When your principal supervisor did try to facilitate from a teaching and learning stance, it was in a way that reflected, at best, a superficial understanding of how to do so.

What accounts for these differences? Weren't all the principal supervisors across these districts similarly charged with supporting principals in becoming stronger instructional leaders? We explore these questions in the next chapter.

CHAPTER 4

Supporting the Supporters

PRINCIPAL SUPERVISOR JUNE WRIGHT sat down with her own supervisor, the associate superintendent of schools, pulled out her learning plan, and began:

> So, last time, we talked about my time and how I feel like I've been spending most of it with my two new principals just getting them going. You asked me to bring any data that we can look at together about how I am using my time. So here's my calendar, which shows I didn't actually cancel any other meetings, but just added more time with my other principals. And then I did a quick exit survey after my last meeting and checked how the group feels about my time, their access to me this year. I got 4s and 5s on that.

The associate superintendent asked, "How do you see the problem now that we're looking at data? Just like how you ask your principals to test their gut with data, I'm asking you."

Wright said she sees that the data paint a different picture of her time—that she has been attentive to both the existing and new principals in her group—but she still feels like she isn't doing enough. The associate superintendent responded:

> This work is a long game. We can't have you burning out or doing too much for the principals, even the new ones. Their teachers need to see them, not you . . . The shifts in Human Resources mean that new principals should be coming in even more ready and not taking too much of your time. If they are, we need to look at that—like what's going on with the new screening. Or maybe we need to look at how we onboard new principals as a district with support for the operational stuff so you can really focus on their instructional leadership.

PRINCIPAL SUPERVISOR MICHELLE DAVIS led a conversation with her principal supervisor colleagues on race-based microaggressions. The group of three principal supervisors had read about the effects of such behaviors on student and adult learning and were discussing the implications for their work with principals. One said, "We've got to do this. Make our equity work actually about equity." He further reflected that the district's emphasis on excellent teaching and learning for each and every student was a start, but that they now needed to "up their game" by helping principals more directly address racism as a barrier to student opportunity and outcomes. Another added:

> These readings are really calling us to task. I've been really race silent in my work with them [my principals]. We talk about gaps and those kids over there. But we need to name it. Those kids are Latino. And not all Latino kids are *the same*. Some are learning English and some can school us in it. Some are newly in the United States, but most aren't. And all this gap talk is really us saying deficits, deficits, deficits: "What *can't* these kids do?" instead of "What are they great at so we can use that?"

PETE LEWIS AND DAN GIL, superintendents in two small, rural districts, sat down with their coffee and their professional learning plans for their monthly feedback session. The two had gotten to know each other well through meetings at their regional central office and bonded over their confusion about how to focus the principal supervision part of their roles on instruction. In Lewis's words, "I just didn't get it. Mine's a small district, but all the examples come from big urbans. We don't have a person for this and someone else for that. I am the principal supervisor and the Human Resources director, but last week I had to fix a school bus. Dan and I got to talking and looking back at the examples, translating them for our world, and we started to want to figure out how to do this work in our small districts."

The two started by reading together about how to provide challenging feedback to principals. Then, they borrowed a template from a larger district and developed a learning plan to help them grow their own instructional leadership with principals. Every month, they meet to give each other feedback. Gil explained, "With this work, it's just good to talk with someone who is going through the same thing. My school board doesn't get this. And my principals didn't either, but then I started being with them more as a coach and a partner and about instruction and they said, kind of, 'Wow, I didn't know it could be like this.' I mean, they always liked me. But now it's like we are falling in love all over again—over instruction!"

What do these examples have in common? Each illustrates specific conditions that we found important to principal supervisors in the positive cases taking a teaching and learning approach. June Wright's own supervisor dedicated time to helping the district's principal supervisors take a teaching and learning approach and took such an approach herself to foster their learning. Michelle Davis, Pete Lewis, and Dan Gil did not rely on professional development opportunities provided by others or accept the long-standing expectations of principal supervision in their districts; instead, they worked closely with colleagues to lead their own growth.

Less visible in these vignettes, all four principal supervisors arrived on the job with prior knowledge conducive to their taking a teaching and learning approach. Wright and Davis had significant professional experiences that reinforced the importance of their taking the new approach, even in circumstances where they received conflicting messages about doing so. Lewis and Gil had limited experience with directly leading for high-quality teaching and learning. But their years of working in small district central offices meant they deeply understood that the old ways of working in which they were so expert were not effective for too many of their students; they were ready to leave the old ways behind.

In this chapter, we elaborate on the conditions that corresponded with the principal supervisors who took a teaching and learning approach to supporting principals' growth as instructional leaders. First, we show that principal supervisors varied within the positive and negative cases in ways that helped us detect conditions that mattered to how principal supervisors went about their work. Namely, principal supervisors in the positive cases either persisted in taking a teaching and learning approach or grew to do so during our study period. Principal supervisors in the negative cases included those who consistently did not take a teaching and learning approach or regressed in the degree to which they did so.

Then, we discuss how hiring people with certain prior knowledge can start principal supervisors off on the right track, but on-the-job conditions can reinforce or interfere with that trajectory. Surprisingly, we did not associate districts' main formal on-the-job support for principal supervisors—outside coaches—with any of the growth cases. Rather, we found that supervisors of principal supervisors (SPSs) support principal supervisors' persistence especially when they themselves model a teaching and learning approach and broker supportive and aligned resources and relationships for principal supervisors throughout the central office. Principal supervisors are important main agents of their own growth when they work together with colleagues to lead their own learning and protect their time. We conclude with a reminder that all of these dynamics unfolded in central offices reinventing principal supervision as part of their broader transformation efforts, which laid an important foundation for the positive cases.

A CLOSER LOOK AT THE POSITIVE AND NEGATIVE CASES

As outlined in table 4.1, the principal supervisors in the negative cases fell into two categories. The twelve "traditional" cases started out just as that label suggests—these principal supervisors took a traditional supervisory approach to their work with principals, and continued to do so throughout our study period despite their districts' investments in shifting their roles. The negative cases also included four instances of "regression." These principal supervisors started out taking a teaching and learning approach, but their engagement in that approach diminished over time and they ultimately regressed to a traditional supervisory approach.

On the positive side, we categorized twenty-two principal supervisors, the largest group of cases, under "persistence." These principal supervisors started out taking a teaching and learning approach and continued to do so, despite various threats to their approach.

TABLE 4.1 Distribution of principal supervisor cases across study districts

	NEGATIVE CASES		POSITIVE CASES	
	TYPE 1: TRADITIONAL	TYPE 2: REGRESSION	TYPE 3: PERSISTENCE	TYPE 4: HIGH GROWTH
DISTRICT	NUMBER OF PRINCIPAL SUPERVISORS			
1A	3		15	
1B	1	2	2	
1C	2	2	2	
2A	3		2	
2B	2			
2C	1			
2D			1	
2E				1
2F				1
Total	12	4	22	2

The positive cases also included two "high growth" principal supervisors, both superintendents, who started out as traditional principal supervisors but grew fairly quickly to take a teaching and learning approach.

SUPPORTIVE CONDITIONS

When we organized conditions by these four categories of principal supervisor practice, some clear patterns emerged. We outline these in table 4.2 and elaborate on them in the following subsections.

Prior Knowledge

Socio-cultural learning theory and other scholarship on learning is clear about the importance of prior knowledge to professional growth. Professionals come to new situations with orienting frames—ways of seeing and understanding who they are, what circumstances they are in, and what to do day-to-day. These frames are often informed by professional training and also by experiences on the job and other aspects of their lives.

TABLE 4.2 Distribution of principal supervisor cases by conditions

		CASES	PRIOR KNOWLEDGE	OUTSIDE COACHING	SPS MENTORING	LEADERSHIP FOR OWN GROWTH
Negative	Type 1: Traditional	5	No	Strong	Weak	No
		7	No	Weak	Weak	No
	Type 2: Regression	4	Yes	Weak	Weak	No
Positive	Type 3: Persistence	5	Yes	Weak	Weak	Yes
		2	Yes	Strong	Weak	Yes
		15	Yes	Weak	Strong	Yes
	Type 4: High growth	2	Yes	Weak	Weak	Yes

The high number of principal supervisors with no change—traditional and persistence—suggests that prior knowledge mattered; most principal supervisors came in with a fairly strong way of understanding their work that other conditions in their transforming central offices did not interrupt. For example, many of the principal supervisors in the positive persistence cases reported that they had years of experience supporting professional learning for teachers and principals from a teaching and learning approach. In one case, a principal supervisor had been a regional superintendent with multiple staff reporting to her. But even before the launch of the central office transformation in her district, she spent significant time coaching her principals on their instructional leadership. Another left the principalship to coach principals on their instructional leadership before assuming her principal supervisor role. One principal supervisor had written a book on his approach to supporting professional learning, while still another was featured in the national media for her strong ability to lead the learning of teachers and other adults.

Similarly, the principals in the traditional cases tended to report that they believed they had secured the principal supervisor position because they had extensive prior experience leading other central office staff, and that the principal supervisor role was an obvious next step toward becoming a superintendent. Several had received their superintendent certificate in programs that they described as teaching them to manage budgets and ensure smooth district operations. A few had been high school principals who saw themselves as good managers of their school communities, but had little experience with supporting adult learning. Two principal supervisors in a larger district expressed frustration that they did not have other central office staff reporting directly to them, because such formal authority would help them ensure that operational staff were responsive to principals.

These findings make intuitive sense and reinforce the importance of hiring people prepared to engage in the new form of principal supervision from day 1. As table 4.1 shows, district 1A had the most positive persistence cases. Perhaps not surprisingly, this district also stood out for significantly shifting its hiring process to align with the new forms of principal supervision. Leaders in this district fully eliminated the long-standing principal supervisor job description and replaced it with new job specifications focused on principals' growth as instructional leaders. One district leader involved in all of the hiring for that new position explained that he carefully selected for people he thought had deep prior knowledge important to persisting in the new roles in a rapidly transforming central office.[1]

Also pointing to the importance of a transformed principal supervisor hiring process to select candidates with the right prior knowledge, the other larger districts (1B, 1C, 2A, and 2B) with a mixed set of principal supervisor cases did not revise their process. One of these districts simply added the responsibility of helping principal supervisors grow as instructional leaders on to their long-standing job description, which ran many pages long and included "other duties as assigned." The principal supervisor team in that district included two veteran school principals with little experience with instructional leadership.

But why did any of the principal supervisors regress? One reason relates to the definition of prior knowledge, which is not simply past job experiences but the mental models that professionals bring to their work. Past work experiences shape mental models, but the duration and quality of those experiences impact the strength of the mental models, as do other experiences. Consistent with this distinction, the principal supervisors in the regression cases presented résumés that indicated they had past experience appropriate to the new form of principal supervision. But since they were relatively new professionals, that experience typically totaled just a few years and likely meant they had relatively fragile mental models to support a teaching and learning approach. Also, their lack of basic knowledge about central office operations may have left them especially conflicted by the various demands on their role as their district's central office transformation initiatives were still getting under way—that is, less able to distinguish when to engage versus buffer themselves from those demands.

This view of the importance of prior knowledge is further supported by a closer look at the two persistence principal supervisors.

Like those in the regression cases, these two had similarly few years as professionals and the principal supervisor role was also their first central office position. However, these two had come up through nontraditional educational pathways involving alternative teacher certification and, in one case, work in and with charter schools. They both assumed the principal supervisor job with strikingly strong worldviews that central offices needed to operate fundamentally differently and better.

And the two cases of high growth? These principal supervisors were superintendents with long tenures in traditional district leadership roles and readily admitted they had little knowledge of high-quality classroom teaching, let alone how to help a principal support those results. But they did have a deep knowledge of traditional central office operations. When they first learned about the new forms of principal supervision, these principal supervisors initially resisted the examples that mainly came from larger school districts. But they also fairly quickly recognized that the long-standing ways of supervising principals did not support the improvement of teaching and learning, which sparked their curiosity about how the new forms of principal supervision could play out well as part of the superintendency in smaller districts. These cases suggest that professionals may experience a tipping point with prior knowledge that runs contrary to new work demands—a point at which they can readily see and understand the limitations of the established ways of working and open themselves up to fundamentally different alternatives.

Still, given how countercultural the new forms of principal supervision were for these pioneering central offices, we assumed that we would see far fewer persistence cases. And on the flip side, we assumed that since the districts were transforming in ways better aligned with the new forms of principal supervision we would see more growth cases and fewer traditional ones. And some conditions on the job must have prompted regression and growth. Therefore, we turned our attention to on-the-job conditions that may have been related to how principal supervisors went about their work.

Outside Coaching

As noted previously, all the districts contracted with an outside organization with a track record of supporting adult learning, though mainly for teachers and school principals. Our conceptual framework suggested that if those outside coaches took a teaching and learning approach with principal supervisors to help principal supervisors in turn take such an approach with their principals, then principal supervisors would grow and persist in doing so. However, we did not find a clear positive relationship between the quality of the outside support and the distribution of principal supervisor cases. In fact, the principal supervisors working with coaches who provided relatively high-quality support demonstrated no growth.

To elaborate, the outside coaches in districts 2A and 2B frequently worked with principal supervisors as a whole group and one-on-one and took a teaching and learning approach. Principal supervisors in these districts typically offered positive reviews of their outside coaches. For instance, one said, "I can see the concrete changes that happen in my regional [principals] meetings as a result of that [coach's] feedback." However, the principal supervisors in these districts essentially ended where they began—with five out of seven not budging from their traditional supervisory approach.

To illustrate the relatively high quality of coaching in district 2A in terms of the consistency of that coaching with our conceptual framework, the main coach working with that district met with the principal supervisors at least twice a month for whole- or small-group sessions specifically designed to help them take a teaching and learning approach to their work. In one session, this coach convened all the principal supervisors at a school for an entire day to offer guidance on how to teach principals to observe classrooms as part of their instructional improvement efforts. The coach began the session with joint work moves, taking an hour for the principal supervisors to grapple with their district's standards defining high-quality classroom teaching and how and why to use the standards to anchor classroom observations. During this discussion, the coach guided the participants through prioritizing particular aspects of the standards to use on their classroom visits and explained the importance of teaching principals to do so in their own work with teachers.

The coach transitioned by making metacognitive comments that next he was going to model for the principal supervisors how to use particular talk moves to deepen principals' understanding of the quality of classroom teaching. The coach said that often supervisors simply ask principals to brainstorm what they would look for as evidence of particular teaching standards but leave the principals' responses unchecked; by contrast, when supervisors press for an explicit connection between look-fors and standards, the principals truly deepen their understanding of what the standards mean and how to detect them during classroom observations.

Then, the coach asked the principal supervisors for one aspect of the classroom they expect to see related to the standard on student engagement. A principal supervisor said she would know if students were engaged if a teacher used a "thumbs up, thumbs down" strategy, asking students to indicate if they understood a concept with the direction of their thumb. The coach then probed with various talk moves. For instance, the coach asked, "How do you relate that to student engagement?" The principal supervisor responded, "It gives all kids an easy way to say whether they are [understanding]." The coach then asked, "Can you calibrate with the [standard] tightly?" explaining that just because teachers were checking for understanding and students were responding, it did not mean that students were actually engaged in ways important to learning. The coach said that the language in the standard about what student engagement looks like could help the principal supervisor assess evidence of student engagement. The coach then asked the other principal supervisors to agree or disagree with that explanation, using the specific language of the standard on student engagement as a jumping-off point.

By contrast, the coaches in the other districts provided lower-quality assistance. Not surprisingly, we found all four of the regression cases in districts that worked with those coaches, but we also found cases of persistence and the two high-growth cases.

To illustrate how these coaches worked, in district 1A, an outside coach with almost twenty years of experience coaching principals convened principal supervisors at least twice a month to discuss written cases of principals' leadership and how to address them. These written cases typically came from real situations that principal supervisors faced, which suggested some consistency with learning through authentic tasks. However, in the meetings we observed, the coach asked principal supervisors to share with one another in small groups how they would approach each case, and then simply moved on to the next task without engaging in the joint work move of reinforcing a clear, common understanding about their role in the cases. Principal supervisors generally reported that the meetings confirmed their own preexisting views, even when those views differed from their charge to support principals' growth as instructional leaders.

In district 1B, outside coaches typically had principal supervisors bring examples of data on each school and helped them discuss what they thought the principal should be doing to improve that school's data. But, across meetings, these discussions rarely focused on how the principal supervisors themselves would help the principal lead for those improvements.

The coaches who worked with the smaller districts (districts 2C–F) convened district leaders for professional learning sessions and also coached the superintendents one-on-one. These coaches framed their work as supporting principal supervisors' learning, but we did not see evidence of those results in practice. For instance, at one session for all four of the districts as well as two others in their learning network, three outside coaches began with moves potentially consistent with metacognitive strategies, as when one coach explained the rationale for each segment of the meeting and how they designed the meeting to help participants realize certain learning targets. But the three coaches then talked at the group for long stretches of the meeting in ways that prompted some principal supervisors to disengage.

For instance, in one segment, a coach posed a question, ostensibly a talk move, to encourage participants to deepen their understanding of how to use a particular protocol for classroom observations. The coach solicited two comments, did not respond to those comments, and then talked to the group for approximately fifteen minutes with only the other two coaches chiming in; this was followed by a seven-minute video and about five more minutes of instructions from one of the coaches. Only then did the coaches ask the participants to engage in small-group discussion about the materials.

During the small-group discussions, many participants did not start the activity. One said she had not paid attention to the instructions; another commented that he had trouble hearing the video. Two coaches then interrupted the small-group discussions to offer further instructions about how the conversation should proceed. The groups we observed generally did not follow the prompts.

These coaches also tended to introduce more ideas and protocols than participants could follow. For instance, one coach opened another meeting by taking over fifteen minutes to list multiple meeting goals, including "aligning to research," "use of tools," "principals' instructional leadership," and "cycle of inquiry." The coach then posed broad questions not obviously tied to the framing comments and directed meeting participants to discuss the questions in their teams. At that point, one principal supervisor commented to a colleague, "I lost her. When she asked us to review those four questions, I started to read them and then she interrupted and from then on I just got scrambled." Another commented, "I'm having a hard time keeping up because the conversation keeps jumping around." A third said, "I need to feel a sense of closure before we jump into the next topic."

In sum, outside coaching varied in its consistency with our conceptual framework, which we used as a marker of quality. Contrary to what our framework suggested, the higher-quality coaching involved principal supervisors who showed no growth. We saw relatively low-quality coaching in the districts with the regression cases, but also with some persistence cases and both the high-growth cases.

We were willing to say that our conceptual framework got it wrong when it came to principal supervisor learning. But first, we reexamined if the outside coaching was *consistent enough* with our conceptual framework. As the previous examples illustrate, during sessions with principal supervisors, the outside coaching we identified as high-quality reflected in-the-moment teaching moves such as modeling and talk. But we did not find evidence that the outside coaches helped principal supervisors lead their own learning. Instead, the coaches had contracts with each district to provide a certain number of days of professional development, and they delivered those days. Across virtually all the professional development sessions between the coach and principal supervisors in district 2A, for example, the coach frequently invited principal supervisors' sense-making about various ideas—a strategy for activating learners' agency. The coach also asked principal supervisors to complete various "homework" assignments, such as trying out a particular strategy with a principal and bringing back evidence of how it went for discussion. But throughout, the coach—not the principal supervisors—was leading the learning. The coach determined the focus and approach of the professional development sessions and facilitated all of them. Similarly, when we observed planning meetings of the two coaching groups working with districts 2A–2F, their conversations focused on how they would organize their learning sessions, not how they were supplementing principal supervisors' efforts to lead their own learning in the ways that socio-cultural learning theories emphasize.

Outside coaches also did not engage in brokering—bridging principal supervisors to the rest of the central office and buffering them from distractions to taking a teaching and learning approach with their principals. The fact that outside coaches did not broker makes sense, since such navigation of the broader central office would likely be quite challenging for an outsider. But the absence of brokering may have mitigated the effects of the rest of the outside coaching support. The lack of brokering meant that the principal supervisors missed out on important resources to support their persistence and growth as well as protection for their time and own learning. Ultimately, by bringing in outside coaching the district was delegating responsibility for principal supervisors' growth to individuals with no formal status or influence within the central office. Such delegation possibly mitigated the extent to which the principal supervisors saw their growth as of value in their districts—a feature of joint work also important to learning.

SPS Mentoring

We then shifted our question from "How did the coaches work?" to "To what extent did the principal supervisors have access to other supports for their own learning?" We found that in the larger systems where chief academic officers or superintendents directly supervised the principal supervisors, those SPSs interacted with principal supervisors in ways that may have mattered to the overwhelming persistence of positive cases in district 1A and the mixed results in the other districts (1B, 1C, 2A, and 2B).[2]

To elaborate, the SPS in district 1A, like Principal Supervisor June Wright's supervisor in the vignette at the start of this chapter, stood out for consistently taking a teaching and learning approach to his work with the district's principal supervisors—modeling how to handle challenging situations, using talk moves, bridging principal supervisors to additional resources for their work with their principals, and buffering them from distractions. In one typical meeting, a principal supervisor asked for the SPS's advice about how to work with a principal on a series of parent complaints the principal had asked the principal supervisor to handle. The SPS modeled thinking by sharing that when such situations come up, he asks himself questions such as, "Will taking on this complaint help the principal engage in instructional leadership?" Through this dialogue, the principal supervisor sorted the complaints into 1) those to turn back to the principal (a form of buffering herself), 2) those to handle personally (a form of buffering the principal), and 3) those that other central office leaders could address (a form of bridging principal supervisors to additional resources to support their instructional focus).

In another instance, the principal supervisor met with the SPS to talk through data that showed one high school principal struggling to support his department heads in leading teacher learning communities. The principal supervisor had not been the principal of a comprehensive high school herself, and said she frequently sought out her

SPS's advice because he had been a high school principal and often had good suggestions. The two talked through the available data and surfaced that the principal actually had had some successes working with two of his department heads when collaborating with his dean of students. The SPS and principal supervisor then role-played how the principal supervisor might have a conversation with the principal to help him make sense of the data himself and identify next steps.

This SPS also encouraged principal supervisors to lead their own learning. For example, the district used an end-of-year survey to solicit principals' detailed feedback on their supervisor. The SPS led the principal supervisors—as a whole group and also in one-on-one meetings—in reflecting together on their survey results. At one such meeting, the SPS used a protocol that asked the principal supervisors to work together in pairs to interpret what they thought their own results meant about their practice and their relationship with their principals, what growth areas they would identify for themselves going into the next year, and some specific steps they would take to succeed with their growth goals.

The SPSs in the other larger systems—districts 1B,1C, 2A, and 2B—talked about their role as supporting principal supervisors' learning. For instance, one said, "I know I make a special effort when [principal supervisors] call me . . . I try to make sure they get what they need as quickly as they can, because the bottom line is providing service to schools. That's it. That's it." The SPSs in one district created "blackout days," or dedicated days of each week when no one in the central office could place demands on principal supervisors or their principals that threatened their focus on principals' instructional leadership.

But the SPSs' execution of these supports was neither extensive nor consistent with the kinds of moves our conceptual framework suggested would support principal supervisors' persistence and growth. For example, district 1B's two SPSs occasionally observed their principal supervisors working with their principals and then provided the principal supervisors with feedback. But the principal supervisors generally reported that the SPSs did not have much experience with principal supervision themselves and rarely provided useful feedback. District 2B sponsored an end-of-year survey of principals about the central office, including their principal supervisor, and several principal supervisors reported that their SPS simply emailed them the results with no follow-up. In district 1B, we observed the SPSs delegating tasks not related to principals' instructional leadership to principal supervisors.

Looking back at table 4.2, why, then, were the seven persistence principal supervisors with weak support from outside coaches and their SPSs able to persist? Was strong prior knowledge all that it took? And what else was going on for the high-growth principal supervisors that they came to take a teaching and learning approach despite having little to no background in instructional leadership, weak outside coaching, and no immediate supervisor of their own who could have served as a coach?

Leadership of Own Growth

In addition to prior knowledge, we found that all principal supervisors in the positive persistence and growth cases frequently took various steps to support their own growth, such as intentionally connecting with potentially helpful colleagues and buffering themselves from distractions. By contrast, the principal supervisors in the negative cases typically did not lead their own learning specifically around taking a teaching and learning approach with their principals.

First, the principal supervisors in the positive cases proactively sought out colleagues to learn with together. For example, a principal supervisor in district 1A reported that she often reached out to "like-minded" colleagues to share their experiences and get advice on their work with principals. A persistence principal supervisor in district 1B said that while the sessions with the outside coaches were not especially useful, she made a point to sit with particular colleagues, and in that way the meetings "contributed to how we operate and understand the role." Like Pete Lewis and Dan Gil, the two superintendents in the high-growth cases sought each other out more frequently over the course of the study to discuss what they were learning with their coaches, as well as what they heard from their principals and teachers about what counts as high-quality instruction. One of them was clear about the importance of his leadership of his own learning. For instance, he explained that the work with the outside coaches exposed him to new ideas in ways that sparked his interest in the new forms of principal supervision. But, he said, "I don't think you want to let it [outside coaching] go on too long. Because the bottom line is whether it's [name] as the coach or somebody else, they're only here X amount of days per year." This principal supervisor went on to describe how he developed and participated in learning communities alongside his principals to increase their collective knowledge of high-quality classroom teaching and learning and principal instructional leadership.

The persistence and high-growth principal supervisors also frequently buffered *themselves* from interferences with their taking a teaching and learning approach—rather than relying on their SPS to do so on their behalf. As one explained:

> Last year I got completely awash in that logistical kind of side-tracking stuff. And so we as [principal supervisors] made a commitment to twenty-four hours in schools focused on instruction every week. And so what I'm doing is, I'm starting to ignore the noninstructional stuff . . . And I don't feel bad about it because I'm really getting feedback, too, from the principals that our time in the schools is truly making a difference for their instructional focus and what they're doing for instruction.

As another of these principal supervisors explained, even in the district with formal blackout days protecting their time with principals, "You have to have the courage to say, 'I can't serve on that committee, can't go to that meeting, can't do that right now. Sorry. Tied up in a school doing my business.'"

Many of these principal supervisors did not simply say no to outside requests but also took steps to minimize them over the long term. For instance, we reviewed a series of emails that began with the central office security staff telling a principal supervisor that one of her principals had moved a cone in the parking lot and that the principal supervisor should tell the principal not to do that anymore. The principal supervisor responded over a series of emails, explaining that her role was to help principals support their teachers, not to communicate messages from the central office. She encouraged the security staff to contact the principal directly or consider letting the matter go. As noted, principal supervisors in district 1A typically brought distractions to the attention of their SPS, who helped them with their efforts to buffer their time.

The principal supervisors in the negative cases did not engage in such behaviors. For instance, when we asked them about supports for their work, including their own growth, these principal supervisors typically pointed to their sessions with their outside coach as their main learning time. Two of these principal supervisors in district 2A with the relatively high-quality coaching seemed particularly disengaged from many of these meetings, frequently not bringing the required homework and arriving late or leaving early to attend other meetings in the central office. Two of the principal supervisors in the regression cases reported that they frequently consulted with colleagues to support their learning—but the focus of those consultations was on basic operations of the central office since they were new to the district and working in a central office role for the first time.

These principal supervisors also did not buffer themselves from demands that took their time away from their work with principals, and in some cases they actively sought out other responsibilities. For instance, on one visit to the central office we ran into a principal supervisor who was leading a series of learning sessions for teachers on antiracist teaching. When we asked her why she chose to do so, she said she just really enjoys it and misses working with teachers.

In sum, we found that prior knowledge, teaching and learning support from SPSs, and principal supervisors' efforts to lead their own learning seemed closely associated with the positive growth and persistence cases. We did not associate even high-quality outside coaching with those positive results, possibly because the approach of outside coaches did not emphasize principal supervisors' leadership over their own learning or help the principal supervisors engage the rest of the central office in ways that SPSs or principal supervisors themselves could.

The latter point brings us back to where we began: all of these dynamics played out in districts whose leaders were redesigning principal supervision as one part of a broader effort to transform their central offices into engines of educational equity. Even in those systems, Wright and others bumped up against other central office systems in HR and elsewhere not yet aligned to their new role. But the changes were in progress. Principal supervisors could see they were not alone and how they fit into and contributed to a broader systemic improvement effort. And the more they did the right work with their principals, the more fuel they provided to other district leaders to drive those broader changes.

As we turn to chapter 5 and implications for district leaders and others, we attend to that full picture. There, we address not just the immediate supports we associated with the positive cases, but the importance of district leaders understanding principal supervisors as *one key piece of a broader strategy* focused on driving principals' growth as instructional leaders in service of excellent teaching and learning for each and every student.

CHAPTER 5

It Takes a System

THE HOTEL BALLROOM was abuzz with ideas. Teams of two to four leaders—including principal supervisors—from districts across the country had gathered as part of a national foundation's initiative to learn about the research on central office transformation and take a deep dive into the parts about principal supervision. As we shared the findings from the research, the principal supervisors in attendance all seemed to agree. "That is what I thought my job was going to be when you hired me," one principal supervisor told her superintendent. Another said, "That's the kind of principal supervisor we all wanted when we were principals." At another table, a chief academic officer and two of her principal supervisors discussed a strategy for introducing the superintendent and the rest of the cabinet to the ideas. A superintendent and executive director of teaching and learning from a small rural district were already mapping out a scope and sequence for their meetings with their five school principals and discussing how to make their instructional leadership work with principals a progressively larger part of their district leadership team meetings.

When the group reconvened the following year to discuss their progress with shifting principal supervision, most publicly told success stories. Leaders from several districts traded job descriptions they had rewritten to align the principal supervisors' role with supporting principals' growth as instructional leaders. Others shared information about an organization of external coaches that was "really making a difference."

But later, in a session just for principal supervisors, challenges arose. The principal supervisors from larger districts started the conversation with one sharing, "Yeah, they redesigned the job description, but it's just a job description and not the day in, day out." Another offered, "Some days I think my bosses jumped into all of this without *really* understanding what they were doing." Many across the room snapped in enthusiastic agreement when another said, "By the time I'm done explaining to my principals and HR why I'm not doing the same old staffing work for them, the day is over!" A fourth summarized, "Was it supposed to be this hard?"

A superintendent from a smaller district chimed in:

> We have as many principals in our district as some of you have principal supervisors. And you could think, "Well, you are in the top job, fix this." But we struggle too with too much on our plate—all the things keeping us from working with our building leaders. And it's the same as you and sometimes bigger. Like, you get the parent complaints that bubble up to you and take you off course. Our parents—and we love them—*all* come to me, in the grocery store, at Rotary. And we don't have the supply of principals and teachers who have this new mind-set around instruction. So it's slow work shifting the thinking of principals too—to know when we are in their building it's not mainly to help them fix the roof anymore or to get all friendly, but to really get down to the business of their instructional leadership.

These principal supervisors are not alone. Their colleagues in other districts likewise told us that the shifts in principal supervision that we describe in this book make intuitive sense. They know that when they help principals complete budget forms, respond to parent complaints themselves, and attend too many meetings in the central office, they are probably not doing the right work. They want to focus their time on supporting principals' growth as instructional leaders as principals' main partners.

But realizing these changes poses challenges. Even when central office leaders hire principal supervisors ready to take a teaching and learning approach, those leaders and their supervisors typically run up against central office systems—in Human Resources, Teaching and Learning, Facilities, and other areas—that have been hardwired over decades around a different form of principal supervision. And school principals, including those who value and welcome their principal supervisors' focus on instructional leadership, sometimes still rely on their principal supervisor to help them with staffing, requisitions for building repairs, and other noninstructional issues.

The experiences of the pioneering districts and others with whom we have worked over the years offer many lessons for districts seeking to make these important and intuitive, but challenging, changes in principal supervision. These lessons call on district leaders to move ahead with the new form of principal supervision and immediate supports for principal supervisors' success. But the lessons also remind district leaders that principal supervision—even in small districts—is one part of a broader complex system that must transform as well to realize their equity goals. For principal supervisors to be successful, districts must move beyond shifts in principal supervisors' job descriptions or efforts focused only on principal supervisors to engage in deeper central office change. In this chapter, we discuss some of those lessons.

First, we offer overarching recommendations for educational leaders within and beyond school district central offices who want to be catalysts for and drivers of the kinds of changes we highlight in this book. Then, we outline strategic steps that specific stakeholders—central office leaders, outside providers, and others—can take to do their part in support of this vital work.

WHAT IT TAKES

Let It Go

The main lesson of these years of research and practice is simple: let go of long-standing forms of principal supervision. Even if district leaders do not yet see the value of the specific alternatives we detail in this volume, we encourage them to consider the following questions:

1. What do our principal supervisors mostly spend their time on?
2. How does spending time on those things meaningfully contribute to a coherent system of support for high-quality teaching and learning for each and every student?
3. To what extent are principal supervisors doing the work of other central office staff in ways that create inequities in how schools are supported and lessen the urgency for the rest of the central office to do better?

When we engage district leaders—and policy makers, philanthropists, and others—with these questions, they invariably reach the same conclusion we did in our research: that few, if any, meaningful results come from principal supervisors working in the traditional ways. They readily discuss how they know well that people grow and thrive not mainly with supervision but with support.

When contemplating these questions, district leaders also come to see that when principal supervisors step in and do the work of other central office staff, they take pressure off the rest of the district to improve. They often recognize that much of that other work principal supervisors have been doing—tracking down requisitions for building repairs, assisting with staffing, and helping with school budgeting—is someone else's responsibility. Some principal supervisors had taken on that work as a short-term strategy to compensate for the inefficient or otherwise weak performance of other staff and systems. But short-term became long-term and, in the process, principal supervisors became part of the problem by enabling those other staff and systems to continue to operate poorly.

Seeing the problem is one thing. Doing something about it is another. Even from district leaders who deeply engage those questions, we hear reasons to delay such as, "Ending the old principal supervisor role makes sense—and we will think about it for next year," or "When we get through this round of budget cuts . . . " We appreciate those real concerns and encourage leaders to consider: Is it ever a bad time to do the right work?

These shifts in principal supervision and other aspects of central office transformation can be cost-neutral if district leaders truly transform—that is, eliminate existing positions and repurpose resources for the new work. Some leaders have realized cost savings. For instance, leaders in one district analyzed the price tag of providing professional development to principals and found many redundancies and inefficiencies. These leaders asked hard questions such as, What if we pooled all those resources as well as the salaries of our principal supervisors and fundamentally rethought how we support principal growth? When they put all those resources on the table for reconsideration, they found they could support the new forms of principal supervision while also adding positions to reduce the caseload of each supervisor—even in a year of budget cuts.

Focus Principal Supervisors on Supporting Principals' Growth as Instructional Leaders from a Teaching and Learning Approach

Our findings are not equivocal about what to replace the district principal supervisory function with: intensive support for principals' growth as instructional leaders that proceeds from a teaching and learning approach. Over a decade into our research on principal supervision, we have come to see our research findings as illustrating a predictable pattern: when principal supervisors do not focus on principals' growth as instructional leaders or do not take a teaching and learning approach, we do not see tangible positive results in that regard; but when they do, we predictably see principal growth. This key finding has endured, even as definitions of instructional leadership have evolved, as well as across districts of various sizes across the country.

Taking a teaching and learning approach does *not* mean that principal supervisors position themselves as the main provider of professional development to principals. We have seen some principal supervisors translate our findings in that way—organizing principals' learning primarily around their visits and designing the content of their principals meetings mainly based on how they and others think principals should spend their time together. That way of working reinforces long-standing district norms in which professional development is something that gets *done to* principals and teachers. That approach does not reflect an understanding that professionals actually grow when they actively lead their own learning and that the foundation of a teaching and learning approach is to foster that leadership—in this case, by using one-on-one visits and principals meetings to supplement and enhance principals' efforts to lead their own growth.

Directly Support Principal Supervisors

Our research and experience highlight another predictable pattern: if districts mainly shift the principal supervisor job description and hire for prior knowledge but do not also intensively support their principal supervisors directly in particular ways, principal supervisors struggle to focus and typically revert to old habits (e.g., filling in for other central office staff and sometimes doing for principals what principals should be doing themselves).

The following list, distilled from our research, captures the supports that district leaders should ensure are in place when they launch their principal supervisor transformation effort, including questions for leaders to consider when designing and implementing those supports. These supports include those we elaborate in chapter 4 as well as the starting conditions in each district, identified in chapter 1, that prompted us to choose them as promising study sites in the first place:

- *Role definitions.* To what extent does our district have a "true definition" of the principalship as instructional leadership and principal supervision as support for that leadership? True definitions are those that clearly spell out expectations for how those professionals should work day-to-day; they do not just add new responsibilities on to long-standing role definitions but recreate those descriptions from scratch with the new instructional focus at the core. True definitions also are actively used throughout the school district, anchoring hiring and professional development and informing how other roles get defined. Leaders also use such definitions to engage community members and school staff in understanding and informing the shifts in the principalship and principal supervision in a systemic effort to build collective value for those shifts and lessen distracting demands on principal supervisors' time.

- *Positional authority.* As we recreate our principal supervisory function, how can we maintain that function at an executive level? Such positional authority can reinforce for principals and others that the central office highly values their growth as instructional leaders. While positional authority is only one source of influence in complex organizations, it can help principal supervisors navigate the central office in service of their instructional leadership focus. When principal supervisors sit on or close to the superintendent's cabinet, they can potentially support alignment between cabinet-level decisions and the day-to-day realities of school principals.
- *Organization of principal groups.* How can our district ensure that principal groups are the right composition to foster learning? The right composition means a manageable number of principals for one-on-one work and a sufficient number for a professional learning community. It also means that group members are working toward a common set of target practices and have a range of expertise among members to increase their opportunities to access various models. Therefore, we recommend grouping principals by school level rather than feeder pattern, given the differences in instructional leadership at elementary, middle, and high school levels. We strongly discourage grouping principals by students' test results. Test scores are not a meaningful indicator of principals' instructional leadership; even if they were, such a grouping strategy would create too homogenous a group for deep learning.

- *Principal supervisor hiring.* How will our district transform the principal supervisor hiring process to ensure the recruitment and selection of candidates with a well-developed understanding of and experience with principal supervision from a teaching and learning approach? Such a process would ensure that principal supervisors bring the right mental models to the work from day 1 and truly understand that working with principals on their growth as instructional leaders is the primary function of principal supervision.
- *Professional learning for principal supervisors.* How will we help our principal supervisors lead their own learning? Such help might productively include instituting new routines for principal supervisors to conduct rigorous self-assessments and develop intentional learning plans to support their growth. Outside coaching could help too—provided it enhances principal supervisors' agency over their own learning. But the benefits of outside coaching may not outweigh the costs, which can include leaving principal supervisors feeling that their own supervisor has outsourced support for their growth to someone else. How will district leaders mitigate those downsides?
- *Supervision of the principal supervisors.* For larger systems: How can we ensure that the leader to whom the principal supervisor reports—the supervisor of principal supervisors (SPS)—actively supports his or her learning? Such support includes mentoring principal supervisors from a teaching and learning approach. SPSs in larger systems have an especially important role to play in brokering—bridging principal supervisors to resources to enhance their focus on principals' growth as instructional leaders and also buffering them from distractions. If you are a superintendent in a smaller district: To what extent is my evaluator, the school board, an important support to me in my efforts to shift how I supervise principals? If important, how will I work with board members to help them understand what I am doing to shift that function and why doing so is centrally important to our district's improvement goals?

Truly Tackle the Rest of the Central Office

Over time, these supports will still prove necessary but not ultimately be sufficient to deepen and sustain the new form of principal supervision. Another predictable pattern from our research and experience is that when central offices aim to transform principal supervision absent other aligned shifts throughout the central office, principal supervisors become exhausted and sometimes frustrated from swimming against the tide of central office business as usual. That pattern leads to principal supervisor burnout, turnover, and, in some cases, regression to traditional forms of principal supervision.

Educational leaders can plan to avoid that disappointing future by engaging in fuller central office transformation. To begin that process, leaders might consider: What is our vision for how an instructionally focused principalship and principal supervision are part of a broader district system that we are reorienting from decades of unstrategically accumulated work to a coherent engine for equity? How can we ensure we do not undertake the shifts in principal supervision and leave the rest of the central office largely unchanged? How can we use the shifts in principal supervision as a strategic opportunity to surface how other parts of our central office get in the way of high-quality teaching and learning and start to address those barriers at their systemic roots?

Don't Stop There

We are also looking to district leaders to lead beyond these recommendations and shine a light on next directions for principal supervision and central office transformation more broadly, especially given new developments in the research and practice of educational equity. In particular, we collected our study data at a time when district equity initiatives focused somewhat generally on districtwide teaching and learning improvements for each and every student and the closing of achievement gaps.

Now, a new wave of district equity initiatives defines equity work more precisely and ambitiously as explicitly antiracist.[1] In this view, general calls for high-quality teaching and learning and principal instructional leadership obscure the specific students—students of color, those receiving supports for English language learning, and those living in low-income families, among others—who historically have been marginalized and grossly underserved in public school systems.[2] We will not realize educational equity without identifying and interrupting long-standing patterns of marginalization and harm toward students due to their race, family income, fluency with English, immigration status, gender identity, and sexuality and also without intentionally and systematically building a district culture that taps such diversity as a fundamental asset.[3]

As these approaches deepen and spread, we would expect to see standards for principal instructional leadership increasingly emphasize the importance of principals taking a critical race approach to their work.[4] In turn, district leaders would charge their principal supervisors with assisting principals in growing their own capacity to use a critical race approach to equity, which likely will involve support from principal supervisors we have not yet seen.

Moving forward, principal supervisors also will do well to address how they may operate as main agents of district systems that promote such discrimination *toward principals* and seek ways to identify and transform those behaviors. As a white male principal supervisor in one of our partnership districts recounted, he had noticed that two of his female African American principals did not seem to open up to him in ways he viewed as important to their growth. After some months of trying, he finally succeeded in getting one of the principals to give him feedback.

The principal explained that she has experienced race- and gender-based discrimination in the district since her first days as a classroom teacher. She provided various examples of how the supervisor himself cut her off or talked over her during principals meetings. She reminded him that he passed over her several times for open principalships for which he recommended white assistant principals.

The principal supervisor told us, "The teaching moves and other advice in the research are really helpful as a new foundation or basis for my work with principals. As I get that footing under me, I also need to figure out how to deal with this whole other layer that makes me ineffective with exactly the leaders I really mean to support."

And in turn, as the number of principal supervisors of color increases, district leaders would also do well to consider the implications of historical inequities for supporting principal supervisors' success. For example, a principal supervisor who identifies as female and Latina reflected that the new forms of principal supervision make great sense to her and that they also present her with particular risks. She explained that women of color in her district have not had many opportunities for advancement, and yet now that she's finally in the central office as a principal supervisor she's supposed to work against long-standing expectations of that role. For years, the largely white male principal supervisors did not have to "disagree with some very important people." But now she is supposed to push up against some of that power, and to do so from a far more vulnerable position than that of her predecessors. How will district leaders ensure that they are promoting leaders of color into principal supervisor roles and also supporting them as they confront traditional principal supervision and central office business as usual?

As district equity initiatives proceed in these promising and challenging directions, district leaders would do well to attend to the following:

- How can we ensure that the definition of the principalship our principal supervisors are supporting emphasizes true educational equity?
- How will our charge to principal supervisors reflect the importance of a teaching and learning approach to helping principals grow as *equity-focused* instructional leaders?
- How will we help our principal supervisors deepen their understanding of how their own positionality and biases are liabilities and assets in their work with principals?
- How will our support for principal supervisors' success reflect our deepening understanding of differences in their leadership

opportunities and experiences based on race, gender, and other identity markers historically associated with marginalization?

WE ARE THE SYSTEM TOO

We organized the preceding sections around general lessons with nods to district leaders. That strategy can highlight main implications and overall next steps for multiple stakeholders, but also can sometimes obscure implications for specific audiences including school principals, outside coaches and support providers, policy makers, foundation leaders, and researchers. What are some of those specific implications?

Principals

Even the school principals who fundamentally see themselves as instructional leaders can struggle with the transition in their principal supervisors' role. Maybe they have come to count on their principal supervisor to help them with operational matters and otherwise shield them from central office inefficiencies. Why should they now let go of that important resource? Or they could feel, like the female African American principal introduced earlier, that they have tried to open up their practice to their principal supervisor in the past but without positive results. Why should they now trust their principal supervisor with their leadership struggles, even when the principal supervisor says he is now there to help? These common and important concerns can create a kind of stalemate scenario: principal supervisors highlighting how they cannot take a teaching and learning approach with unwilling principals, and principals saying they need to see evidence of principal supervisors' taking on their new role before they will deeply engage.

These dynamics make sense. And principal supervisors should take the lead as part of their joint work moves—relentlessly reinforcing the value of the new promised relationship with principals—as should SPSs and other district leaders throughout the rest of the central office. Principals can also break the stalemate sooner and otherwise proactively advance their relationship with their principal supervisor.

As a basic first step, consistent with leading their own learning, principals can request from their principal supervisor early support that is especially likely to help them build trust while they work together on principals' growth as instructional leaders. For instance, one principal told her supervisor that for years she had tried to open up her practice to her supervisor but that doing so had become too risky, especially in light of the progressively sharper stakes tied to the principal evaluations her supervisor still had to complete. She explained to her supervisor that she builds trust with people by learning alongside them. She asked that for their first year they focus their time together like the principal and supervisor featured in chapter 2—who worked together with a coach so they both could grow in particular shared target areas (in that case, in their knowledge of leadership for high-quality mathematics instruction). Another principal asked her supervisor if they could check in together quarterly to talk openly about how their relationship was going and how to make midcourse corrections.

Principals can also resist making "old" requests of their principal supervisors. For instance, though principals may have done so in the past, they should no longer ask their principal supervisor for help with personnel matters that they are supposed to handle themselves or refer to someone in HR. Over time, those kinds of requests erode principal supervisors' focus on instructional leadership and take pressure off other parts of the central office to work better. Principals have important roles to play in keeping that pressure on. In fact, one of the most significant curbs on central office change is how the ineffectiveness of various central office functions gets normalized as "just the way it is"—especially by long-time principals and central office staff who have come to have low expectations of their central office colleagues and to rely on work-arounds. Principals can avoid being a part of the normalization problem by not overrelying on their principal supervisor and expecting more and better support from their central office.

Principals can also provide their supervisor with meaningful, detailed feedback on *their* areas of strength and those that need improvement, especially since principals should have the best seats in the house when it comes to seeing and experiencing how principal supervisors work. Just as principal supervisors should be working with their principals on how to provide them with feedback, principals too can engage their supervisors in planning for how principals, individually and a group, will provide their supervisors with important data about their practice that they can then use to lead their own learning. Such strategies can include codeveloping protocols for collecting feedback after each principals meeting and advising on the construction of an annual survey. (See exhibit 2 for one resource.)

Outside Coaches

Our research also has several specific implications to help outside coaches, and other staff of intermediary and school support organizations, ensure they are adding value to districts' efforts to improve the performance of their principal supervisors. First, leaders of such organizations can build their capacity to support the learning of principal supervisors in ways that reflect the dynamics and demands of that particular role. In our study and partnership districts, we have seen many outside organizations take their strategies and tools from working with teachers and principals and simply use them more or less as is with principal supervisors—with limited success. Or they teach principal supervisors how they as outside coaches support principals' learning, even though coaching a principal from a longstanding supervisory position within a district central office presents different opportunities and challenges than outside coaches typically face. How can outside organizations avoid these missteps and create more effective and relevant supports for principal supervisors?

In the process, leaders of outside organizations would do well to remember that their staff may be skilled at teaching moves such as modeling, metacognition, and other staples of professional coaching models, but a teaching and learning approach starts with activating and deepening learners' agency over their own learning. Such an emphasis is especially important given that outside coaches cannot spend the amount of time with principal supervisors that a true job-embedded approach requires; if principal supervisors are going to continuously improve, they must intentionally seek out other learning opportunities. How can outside organizations help principal supervisors develop the routines and daily practices important to leading their own learning—especially when doing so means principal supervisors will decrease their reliance on outside coaches and some of those coaches will essentially be working themselves out of a job?

Policy Makers and Philanthropic Leaders

As we note in chapter 1, building school district central office capacity to lead for equity-focused teaching and learning improvement has not been a long-standing investment area for federal and state policy makers, nor has it been for private philanthropic foundations. But research and experience continue to demonstrate the importance of central office leadership for those results, and policy makers and philanthropic leaders can help support such leadership.

First, policy makers and philanthropic leaders can build on the research and experience we share here suggesting that strategic points of investment include principal supervisors as main supporters of principals' instructional leadership growth. Such investments could address: time and other resources to help principal supervisors lead their own learning; learning opportunities for SPSs to understand their key role in principal supervisor support; and, ultimately, support for transforming other central office functions in ways consequential to the success of principals and their supervisors.

Policy makers and philanthropic leaders also can help districts stay the course. This new form of principal supervision, and central office transformation more broadly, is about remaking the basic fabric of the central office bureaucracy so that specific reforms—such as equity policies, math initiatives, and social-emotional learning, among others—rest on the right foundation for their success. When it comes to fundamental change like this, circumstances may get worse before they improve. How can policy makers and philanthropic leaders help central office leaders move continuously forward, especially when faced with setbacks? And how can they too trust in district leaders' transformative work, even during such difficult times? Maintaining momentum may require extending grant periods beyond what those policy makers and philanthropic leaders have traditionally funded and placing new value on leading indicators of change (such as shifts in central office roles) instead of mainly lagging indicators (such as improved student learning).

Moving continuously forward also means addressing not one central office function, such as principal supervision, but rather how various central office functions—hiring, professional development, school improvement planning, and data among them—are interrelated; changes in just one function, such as principal supervision, invariably run up against other systems that are not yet aligned with those changes. Policy makers and philanthropic leaders can help districts interrupt this cycle of unsuccessful, siloed change strategies by focusing their support in ways that address central office interdependencies. For instance, a grant for principal supervisor improvement could also require and provide funds for planning and implementation of aligned changes in HR and principal professional development by other units.

Policy makers and philanthropic leaders also can support the ongoing generation and use of new knowledge to guide central office improvement efforts. If such knowledge is truly going to point the way to educational equity, research must move beyond school-level studies to reveal the deeply institutionalized systemic roots of educational inequities in central offices. Such research would address not just the central office sources of inequities but also how to uproot and reinvent district systems as engines of educational equity. In our own work, we have benefited from funding that provided us with the flexibility and support this work requires. We encourage policy makers and philanthropic leaders to continue and expand those knowledge-building opportunities, such as leveraging research-practice partnerships to help districts use the ideas about principal supervision and central office leadership advanced here to deepen and extend the research findings. Given the vast amount of data generated in such studies, funders could ensure that researchers have the time necessary to truly mine their data and generate knowledge resources for the field.

Researchers

We know well that researchers too are a part of the system that has only begun to contribute to central office progress and could be better marshaled as a key support moving forward. Researchers can help, in part, by taking a strengths-based approach—focusing on what central offices do when they help, rather than hinder, educational equity and other school improvement initiatives.

Our own work suggests that such dynamics are difficult to see without researchers deeply engaging with central office leaders. For instance, our methods have included walking busy central office leaders to their cars to squeeze an additional five or ten minutes out of an interview, talking with them by phone on their commutes home, reading their emails (with permission, of course), shadowing them throughout their day, and otherwise putting ourselves in places where we could see their work unfold in real time. That level of involvement with central office leadership practice will challenge some researchers who are more accustomed to holding central offices at arm's length and relying on one-time interviews rather than observations as their main data sources.

When researchers do study central offices, they tend to do so in silos—looking just at principal supervision, or central office leadership of math reform, or the implementation of particular funding policies, for example. But as we have noted, a key lesson from our research on principal supervisors, and central office transformation more broadly, is that those central office silos are actually interconnected and depend on one another to grow and change. If we had only looked at principal supervisors without also understanding those other central office systems, we may have missed important aspects of principal supervisors' work and how to support it. How might research moving forward broaden its unit of analysis to capture such interdependent daily realities in school district central offices?

Research also would do well to build on what we have already learned about transforming central offices to address critical gaps in the field. The transforming central offices we have studied offer important foundational lessons that researchers and others can use as a jumping-off point for building new knowledge about how every central office function must work both independently and together as a coordinated system to support true educational equity. Again, the right kinds of partnerships between researchers and practitioners can help get extant research into use and support districts in building upon it to design better approaches to principal supervision and central office leadership more broadly.

Ultimately, taking next steps will require educational leaders of all stripes to resist becoming overwhelmed by the scope of the changes we describe here with words like "fundamental" and "transformation." There could always be a better time for such changes, but also, as we have underscored, there is never a wrong time to do the right work. Policy initiatives now abound that aim to address teaching and learning quality and educational equity. But we still see little sustained attention to redesigning the district systems on which the success of those initiatives relies, and therefore too many of the initiatives falter and ultimately fold. Moving forward, district leaders serious about educational equity must attend to the deeply rooted mismatch between the central office systems we have and those we need to truly improve teaching and learning at scale for each and every student, especially those students whom public school systems have persistently marginalized and underserved.

Focusing principal supervisors on principals' growth as instructional leaders is one potentially high-leverage way to begin. When principal supervisors dedicate themselves to helping principals grow as instructional leaders from a teaching and learning approach, they shift the relationship between the central office and schools from operations, compliance, and evaluation toward a partnership in service of principal, teacher, and student success. Such partnerships advance the development of principals, principal supervisors, and other educational leaders as true professionals—equipping them with the supports they need to lead their own learning and to work together effectively for real results. As districts use these ideas, the efforts of June Wright and the other principal supervisors we feature in this book become the rule rather than the exception and build meaningful momentum behind the right work.

APPENDIX

Tools You Can Use

When we share the research and experience that ground this book, principal supervisors often ask us, "Do you have any tools we can use—especially ones that could help us focus our work on principals' growth as instructional leaders, take a teaching and learning approach, or deepen principals' and others' understanding of our new role?" That question makes a lot of sense. Whole industries have built up to support high-quality teaching and principal leadership. But, as we note in chapter 1, if you are a principal supervisor—or an SPS or in some other central office position—resources specifically designed to support your central office work are few and far between.

To address that gap in the field, over the past few years we have developed several materials specifically to support principal supervisors in leading their own learning to take a teaching and learning approach to their work, including:

- Principal supervisor performance standards against which principal supervisors and others can continuously assess their progress.[1] (See exhibit 1.)
- Survey instruments to provide principal supervisors and others with data about principal supervisors' growth.[2] (See exhibit 2.)

- A professional growth planning process to help principal supervisors use standards and various data to develop and implement their own learning plans.[3] (See exhibit 3.)

In this appendix, we discuss these resources and how to use them. We also provide questions you can use to reflect on and discuss the ideas in this book. (See exhibit 4.)

Importantly, we have found that the most useful tools for principal supervisors, and those who support them, are not the ones outsiders like us design and district leaders simply adopt. Rather, when leaders of complex change processes work from ideas and examples to author or design materials *for themselves*, they come to deeply understand and own those resources. This observation makes sense in light of the importance of agency to learning, which we emphasize throughout this book.

For example, one district with five principal supervisors spent several weeks over the summer reviewing and making sense of our principal supervisor performance standards, as well as the principal supervisor standards of two other organizations, to help them identify a set of standards that resonated with them. A small-district superintendent worked with colleagues who led other districts to clarify how each standard applied to them as superintendents and supervisors. They ended up agreeing that the first standard about time would mean they would spend 30 percent of each week working directly with principals on their instructional leadership in the first year, possibly increasing to 50 percent the next year for superintendents with eight or more principals. They rewrote the sixth standard about engagement with the rest of the central office to focus them on their active leadership of the transformation of the rest of the central office outside the 30–50 percent they spent with principals.

The SPS in another district took our survey instruments and added and amended items to make the content especially relevant in his setting. As a strategy to help principal supervisors increase ownership over their growth, the chief academic officer in a midsized district gave her supervisors an editable version of our professional growth planning process and asked them to rewrite it as though they were creating it for themselves.

Informed by these and other examples, next we present each tool in an effort to spark principal supervisors' interest in actively adopting, editing, or otherwise coming to own the tools in ways that make sense to them. To support principal supervisors in such authorship or design processes, we introduce each tool by first describing why it can help principal supervisors lead their own learning. Second, we identify specific design features we recommend that each tool reflect. Third, we offer an example of each tool that includes those features. To conclude, we suggest ways principal supervisors and others can use this volume as a support for their persistence and growth.

TOOLS FOR PRINCIPAL SUPERVISORS' CONTINUOUS IMPROVEMENT

Principal Supervisor Performance Standards

Performance standards provide clear images of the new forms of principal supervision that principal supervisors can use to focus their efforts to lead their own learning, monitor their own progress, and reinforce for their principals and others what they should expect of them. When principal supervisors adopt common standards with other principal supervisors, they strengthen their ability to work together as a team toward a shared vision of their work.

Whichever standards principal supervisors choose, we recommend that those standards reflect the following design features, which are important to ensuring that the standards can function in those ways and otherwise support principal supervisors' growth.

- *Research-based.* Make sure the standards rest on robust evidence showing that working in the ways the standards describe is likely to support principals' growth as instructional leaders. Otherwise, principal supervisors are likely to diffuse their efforts in areas not proven to be effective in ways that matter most.

- *Measurable.* Standards are not especially useful learning tools unless learners can assess how much they are growing along each standard. Some professional standards include dispositions or attitudes, but those attributes are generally hard to measure. They also use scales such as "beginner" to "proficient," without sufficient definitions of each level of practice. Instead, focus your principal supervisor standards on observable practices associated with positive results. Use a self-assessment scale, such as the degrees of appropriation, to capture measurable markers of how people progress to deeper practice.
- *Usable.* Standards help guide professional practice when users feel like they understand, value, and own them. Standards are also especially useful when they help learners focus—that is, when they call professionals' attention to particularly important aspects of their practice to ground their learning. Therefore, even when using standards developed by an outside organization, engage principal supervisors in grappling deeply with what the standards mean and why each is important. Also, ensure that the standards are a manageable number for focusing, rather than diffusing, principal supervisors' attention.

Exhibit 1 includes a set of standards we developed that meet these criteria. Each standard stems from research on how principal supervisors work when their work matters for real results in principals' instructional leadership. We organized the standards around practices that principal supervisors and others can measure using observations as well as surveys, interviews, and analyses of calendars and other documents.[4]

In terms of usability, we reviewed earlier rounds of these standards with over one hundred practitioners to ensure they represented our research findings in ways that resonated with principal supervisors and other central office leaders. An earlier set of these standards was further vetted as part of the Council of Chief State School Officers' national engagement process for codifying national principal supervisor standards.[5]

Still, standards are only as useful as actual principal supervisors find them. Consider some of the strategies we mentioned previously and others for encouraging principal supervisors to grapple deeply with what each standard means, why it offers an important anchor for their practice, and how to use it actively and productively moving forward.

Annual Surveys of Principals and Principal Supervisors

One of the clearest points of consensus in learning theories across fields is that learning requires feedback. However, as we discussed in chapter 1, if you are a central office staff person of any kind, including a principal supervisor, chances are you have access to little or no systematic feedback. Several of our pioneering districts productively used end-of-year surveys of principals for this purpose. (See chapter 4.) Surveys can be relatively quick data collection tools that provide consistent information for comparisons over time. They are especially useful supports if designed properly, taken by the right people, and used alongside other information. Accordingly, we recommend that districts use surveys that meet the following design criteria.

- *Ask the right questions of the right people.* Much of what principal supervisors do is not visible beyond their principals, their principal supervisor colleagues, and their own supervisors. Resist the temptation to survey other people and tailor your survey questions to each type of respondent.
- *Ensure items are valid and reliable.* These basic qualities of good surveys remind us to construct survey items that are valid (that is, they measure what we want them to) and that they produce reliable results (that is, survey takers understand survey terms in the same ways and their responses accurately reflect their experiences or opinions).
- *Don't evaluate survey results in isolation.* While surveys have benefits of efficiency and consistency, they also have limitations when it comes to capturing daily practice. As with other opinion and self-report data, survey responses may reflect various biases, including the tendency of novices to rate their practices higher

than those with more experience and understanding of what the practices entail. Therefore, be sure to consider survey responses alongside other information, such as observations by multiple observers or other data and evidence.

Exhibit 2 includes items from two surveys we developed that meet those design criteria. We tailored these surveys for the two groups who should have some basis for commenting on principal supervisors' performance over time: school principals and principal supervisors themselves. We based these survey items on the performance standards we share in exhibit 1. Over four years, we conducted validity and reliability checks with practitioners, other experts, and survey designers across the country. We encourage principal supervisors and their SPSs to compare results between the surveys to gauge the extent to which their principals and their principal supervisors are on the same page about how they work together.

Professional Growth Planning Process

A carefully structured professional growth planning process (PGPP) can support principal supervisors and other professionals in using survey and other data to lead their own learning toward their own and their districts' performance goals. Such a process can enable principal supervisors to identify target areas, access resources that are especially likely to help them grow in these areas, and make evidence-based reflections on their progress with routine parts of their daily work. When principal supervisors develop and use similar processes that prompt them to collaborate on the design and implementation of their learning plans, they increase their opportunities to work together in support of their professional growth.

Whether principal supervisors choose an existing PGPP or develop their own, their process should reflect research on adult learning, such as socio-cultural learning theory, that identifies practices and conditions to help professionals truly deepen their work. As a starting point, a principal supervisor's PGPP should reflect the following design criteria:

- *Prompt the active use of standards and multiple forms of evidence.* Professionals' assessments of their own performance are typically riddled with biases that may lead them to overestimate or downplay what they know and can do. We can increase the accuracy of the self-assessments that anchor learning planning when we start from clear standards of our professional practice and work from multiple sources of evidence to characterize our current progress along each standard.
- *Move beyond goal setting to develop a specific learning plan.* School districts commonly ask leaders, teachers, and others to set professional goals to guide their growth but not also to spell out what they will actually do to progress toward those goals. When we spell out the intentional steps of what we will do to grow toward our professional goals, those goals become more actionable and likely to produce the results.
- *Focus on opportunities to lead learning while doing.* Research shows that adults improve their practice by learning on the job, yet professional development in school districts is typically oriented to pull adults out of their work for "sit-and-get" professional development provided by someone else. Strong learning plans reflect that research and mostly involve on-the-job learning opportunities, such as having a colleague observe a principal supervisor working with principals and then provide feedback.
- *Prompt collaboration with others.* Learning that shifts practice is fundamentally social as learners see others in practice, talk with one another about new ideas and their own practice, and otherwise together make sense of their experiences in ways that can shift and strengthen mental models to guide ongoing practice. Regular, intentional collaboration with colleagues can help us collect evidence important to our self-assessments, provide a sounding board for our interpretation of our performance data, and provide access to new resources for our learning.

Exhibit 3 includes an outline of a professional growth planning process that reflects these design criteria. This PGPP prompts principal supervisors to start by collecting concrete evidence to self-assess against performance standards. Then, principal supervisors work through a series of prompts to prioritize their growth goals and identify corresponding learning supports—with an emphasis on those they can access on the job. Throughout, the process asks principal supervisors to consult with colleagues to strengthen their plans.

Principal supervisors may also adapt this tool for use with their principals. For instance, one principal supervisor engaged one of her principals with a version of the PGPP that they used together. They each inserted their own performance standards—for principal supervisors and principals—and then each used the process to lead their own growth. Afterward the principal supervisor further adapted the tool and explored using the adaptation with a broader group of principals.

QUESTIONS FOR REFLECTION AND DISCUSSION

Our main impetus for writing this volume was to provide a relatively comprehensive resource for district leaders to help them build on the lessons learned in other districts about principal supervisors. When we reflect on how we and others learn with books, we are reminded of the importance of reading reflectively and sometimes skeptically, asking, "Do I really agree with that? What's an even better idea?" We also appreciate returning to some books we already read to see what we may have missed and what we may now understand differently or better.

To support that kind of critical, continuous improvement process, we conclude this book with exhibit 4. There, we offer sample chapter-by-chapter reflection and group discussion questions to support your use of this volume as an active learning resource. We hope these questions and the examples throughout this volume help you expand your imagination of what's possible in your setting. We also hope that they offer some impetus and inspiration to stay the course, as they have for us in continuing to learn with and from district leaders how to ensure excellent teaching and learning for each and every student, every day.

EXHIBIT 1

Principal Supervisor Performance Standards

DL2 Principal Supervisor (PS) Performance Standards 3.0

STANDARD 1. Dedicates their time to helping principals grow as instructional leaders.

STANDARD 2. Works intensively with principals to help them lead their own growth as instructional leaders.

STANDARD 3. Uses teaching-and-learning moves when working with principals one-on-one to support principals' growth as instructional leaders.

STANDARD 4. Uses teaching-and-learning moves when leading principal communities of practice (e.g., professional learning communities, networks), to support principals' growth as instructional leaders.

STANDARD 5. Engages principals in the formal district principal evaluation process in ways that support principals' growth as instructional leaders.

STANDARD 6. Selectively and strategically participates in other central office work processes to maximize the extent to which they and principals focus on principals' growth as instructional leaders.

Not adopting: Does not yet talk about their practice or engage in practices consistent with the standard.

Adopting the talk: Talks about their practice in ways consistent with the standard, but actual practice does not yet reflect the standard.

Engaging at a surface level: Practice begins to reflect the standard, but does not yet demonstrate deep understanding of which practices are consistent with the standard or why to engage in those practices.

Engaging with understanding:
(1) Practice often reflects the standard and demonstrates deepening understanding of what practices are consistent with the standard and why to engage in those practices.
(2) Practices consistent with the standard are a regular part of daily practice.

Mastery:
(1) Practice routinely reflects the standard at the level of "engaging with understanding" across multiple contexts and years.
(2) Practice across settings and over time demonstrates the ability to improvise—to use the standard as a jumping-off point to develop new ways of working consistent with the standard and likely to contribute to progressively more powerful results.

STANDARD 1 Dedicates their time to helping principals grow as instructional leaders.

NOT ADOPTING	ADOPTING THE TALK	ENGAGING AT A SURFACE LEVEL	ENGAGING WITH UNDERSTANDING	MASTERY
A PS who works at this level does not yet talk about their work as dedicated to supporting principals' growth as instructional leaders or spend time on such activities.	A PS who works at this level talks about their work as dedicated to supporting principals' growth as instructional leaders, but they do not actually spend time on such activities.	A PS who works at this level: • Begins to dedicate some of their time on supporting principals' growth as instructional leaders but does not yet fully dedicate their time to this focus. They frequently engage in work that does not obviously support principals' growth as instructional leaders. • Begins to demonstrate that they understand *what* is entailed in dedicating their time to supporting principals' growth as instructional leaders. • Begins to demonstrate they understand *why* dedicating their time to supporting principals' growth as instructional leaders matters to those results.	A PS who works at this level: • Maximizes their time on principals' growth as instructional leaders. • Makes decisions about how to spend their time based on the extent to which the activity will help them dedicate their time to supporting principals' growth as instructional leaders. • Regularly demonstrates that they understand *how to* dedicate their time to support principals' growth as instructional leaders. • Regularly demonstrates that they understand *why* dedicating their time to supporting principals' growth as instructional leaders matters to those results.	A PS who works at this level: • Demonstrates performance at the level of "engaging with understanding" across multiple contexts and years. • Improvises—uses the standard as a jumping-off point to develop new strategies for dedicating their time to supporting principals' growth as instructional leaders.

STANDARD 2 Works intensively with principals to help them lead their own growth as instructional leaders.

NOT ADOPTING	ADOPTING THE TALK	ENGAGING AT A SURFACE LEVEL	ENGAGING WITH UNDERSTANDING	MASTERY
A PS who works at this level does not yet work intensively with principals to help them lead their own learning as a main support for principals' growth as instructional leaders.	A PS who works at this level reports that they routinely work with principals to help them lead their own learning. However, they do not yet take this approach in their actual practice.	A PS who works at this level: • Begins to work with principals to help them lead their own learning as a main support for principals' growth as instructional leaders. • Begins to demonstrate understanding of *what* is involved in helping principals lead their own learning as a main support for principals' growth as instructional leaders. • Begins to demonstrate understanding of *why* helping principals lead their own learning as a main support for principals' growth as instructional leaders matters to those results.	A PS who works at this level: • Works intensively with principals to help them lead their own learning as a main support for principals' growth as instructional leaders. • Demonstrates a deepening understanding of *what* is involved in intensively working with principals to help them lead their own learning as a main support for principals' growth as instructional leaders. • Demonstrates a deepening understanding of *why* working intensively with principals to help them lead their own learning as a main support for principals' growth as instructional leaders matters to those results.	A PS who works at this level: • Demonstrates performance at the level of "engaging with understanding" across multiple contexts and years. • Improvises—uses the standard as a jumping-off point to develop new ways of working with principals to help them lead their own learning as a main support for principals' growth as instructional leaders.

STANDARD 3 Uses teaching-and-learning moves when working with principals one-on-one to support principals' growth as instructional leaders.

NOT ADOPTING	ADOPTING THE TALK	ENGAGING AT A SURFACE LEVEL	ENGAGING WITH UNDERSTANDING	MASTERY
A PS who works at this level typically directs principals, monitors principals' compliance, or completes tasks that principals should be doing themselves.	A PS who works at this level talks about using teaching-and-learning moves when working with principals one-on-one to support principals' growth as instructional leaders, but they do not yet do so in their actual practice.	A PS who works at this level: • Begins to use teaching-and-learning moves when working with principals one-on-one to support principals' growth as instructional leaders. • Begins to demonstrate they understand *what* is involved in using teaching-and-learning moves when working with principals one-on-one to support principals' growth as instructional leaders. • Begins to demonstrate that they understand *why* using teaching-and-learning moves when working with principals one-on-one to support principals' growth as instructional leaders matters to those results.	A PS who works at this level: • Regularly uses teaching-and-learning moves when working with principals one-on-one to support principals' growth as instructional leaders. • Demonstrates a deepening understanding of *what* is involved in using teaching-and-learning moves when working with principals one-on-one to support principals' growth as instructional leaders. • Demonstrates a deepening understanding of *why* using teaching-and-learning moves when working with principals one-on-one to support principals' growth as instructional leaders matters to those results.	A PS who works at this level: • Demonstrates performance at the level of "engaging with understanding" across multiple contexts and years. • Improvises—uses the standard as a jumping-off point to develop new ways of using teaching-and-learning moves when working with principals one-on-one to support principals' growth as instructional leaders.

STANDARD 4 Uses teaching-and-learning moves when leading principal communities of practice (e.g., professional learning communities, networks), to support principals' growth as instructional leaders.

NOT ADOPTING	ADOPTING THE TALK	ENGAGING AT A SURFACE LEVEL	ENGAGING WITH UNDERSTANDING	MASTERY
A PS who works at this level does not yet convene their principals in meetings that operate as communities of practice devoted to supporting principals' growth as instructional leaders.	A PS who works at this level talks about using teaching-and-learning moves when working with principals in groups to support principals' growth as instructional leaders, but they do not yet do so in their actual practice.	A PS who works at this level: • Begins to use teaching-and-learning moves when leading principal groups to support principals' growth as instructional leaders. • Begins to demonstrate they understand *what* is involved in using teaching-and-learning moves when leading principal groups to support principals' growth as instructional leaders. • Begins to demonstrate that they understand *why* using teaching-and-learning moves when leading principal groups to support principals' growth as instructional leaders matters to those results.	A PS who works at this level: • Regularly uses teaching-and-learning moves when leading principal groups to support principals' growth as instructional leaders. • Demonstrates a deepening understanding of *what* is involved in using teaching-and-learning moves when leading principal groups to support principals' growth as instructional leaders. • Demonstrates a deepening understanding of *why* using teaching-and-learning moves when leading principal groups to support principals' growth as instructional leaders matters to those results.	A PS who works at this level: • Demonstrates performance at the level of "engaging with understanding" across multiple contexts and years. • Improvises—uses the standard as a jumping-off point to develop new ways of using teaching-and-learning moves when leading principal groups to support principals' growth as instructional leaders.

STANDARD 5 Engages principals in the formal district principal evaluation process in ways that support principals' growth as instructional leaders.

NOT ADOPTING	ADOPTING THE TALK	ENGAGING AT A SURFACE LEVEL	ENGAGING WITH UNDERSTANDING	MASTERY
A PS who works at this level engages with the formal district principal evaluation process from a compliance and traditional supervisory approach inconsistent with supporting principals' growth as instructional leaders.	A PS who works at this level talks about engaging principals in the formal district principal evaluation process in ways that support principals' growth as instructional leaders. However, they do not yet take this approach in their actual practice.	A PS who works at this level: • Begins to engage principals in the formal district principal evaluation process in ways that support principals support principals' growth as instructional leaders. • Begins to demonstrate that they understand *what* is involved in engaging principals in the formal district principal evaluation process in ways that support principals' growth as instructional leaders. • Begins to demonstrate that they understand *why* to engage principals in the formal district principal evaluation process in ways that support principals' growth as instructional leaders.	A PS who works at this level: • Regularly engages principals in the formal district principal evaluation process in ways that support principals' growth as instructional leaders; completes evaluation reports as a by-product of teaching-and-learning-focused engagements with principals. • Demonstrates a deepening understanding of *what* is involved in engaging principals in the formal district principal evaluation process in ways that support principals' growth as instructional leaders. • Demonstrates a deepening understanding of *why* to engage principals in the formal district principal evaluation process in ways that support principals' growth as instructional leaders.	A PS who works at this level: • Demonstrates performance at the level of "engaging with understanding" across multiple contexts and years. • Improvises—uses the standard as a jumping-off point to develop new ways of engaging principals in the formal district principal evaluation process to support principals' growth as instructional leaders.

STANDARD 6 Selectively and strategically participates in other central office work processes to maximize the extent to which they and principals focus on principals' growth as instructional leaders.

NOT ADOPTING	ADOPTING THE TALK	ENGAGING AT A SURFACE LEVEL	ENGAGING WITH UNDERSTANDING	MASTERY
A PS who works at this level does not yet approach their work with the rest of the central office selectively or strategically. Instead, they engage with work processes that do not maximize the extent to which they support principals' growth as instructional leaders.	A PS who works at this level talks about how they selectively and strategically participate in other central office work processes to maximize the extent to which they support principals' growth as instructional leaders. However, they do not yet take this approach in their actual practice.	A PS who works at this level: • Begins to selectively and strategically participate in other central office work processes to maximize the extent to which they support principals' growth as instructional leaders. • Does not yet consistently reflect that they understand *what* is involved in selectively and strategically participating in other central office work processes to maximize the extent to which they support principals' growth as instructional leaders. • Does not yet consistently reflect that they understand *why* they should selectively and strategically participate in other central office work processes to maximize the extent to which they support principals' growth as instructional leaders.	A PS who works at this level: • Selectively and strategically participates in other central office work processes to maximize the extent to which they support principals' growth as instructional leaders. • Demonstrates a deepening understanding of *what* is involved in selectively and strategically participating in other central office work processes to maximize the extent to which they support principals' growth as instructional leaders. • Demonstrates a deepening understanding of *why* they should selectively and strategically participate in other central office work processes to maximize the extent to which they support principals' growth as instructional leaders.	A PS who works at this level: • Demonstrates performance at the level of "engaging with understanding" across multiple contexts and years. • Improvises—uses the standards as a jumping-off point to develop new ways of selectively and strategically participating in other central office work processes to maximize the extent to which they support principals' growth as instructional leaders.

EXHIBIT 2

Survey Questions for Principals and Principal Supervisors

This attachment includes question items districts can use to survey the two groups who should be most knowledgeable about principal supervisors' work: school principals and principal supervisors themselves. We provide sample items for principals, organize the items by research-based construct and scale, and encourage districts to adapt each item they use for principal supervisors (specific directions below). By asking both principals and principal supervisors to respond to similar items district leaders can triangulate their responses—or compare the extent to which principals and principal supervisors are on the same page about their work together. The questions about supports in the principal supervisor survey can help district leaders ensure that they are setting their principal supervisors up for success.

As district leaders use these and other items to develop their surveys, we recommend they consider:

- *Tailoring the definition of instructional leadership.* The survey items frequently use the phrase "instructional leadership"—which can mean different things in different districts. District leaders can strengthen the validity of their surveys if they provide a definition of instructional leadership in their survey instructions and adapt items below, where appropriate, to focus on their own definition of instructional leadership. For example, questions about each of the teaching-and-learning moves ask about elements of instructional leadership that we derived from a systematic review of research on principal instructional leadership. District leaders can amend those items to reflect the definition of instructional leadership that they actively use in their settings.

- *Localizing terminology.* District leaders can further improve validity by aligning other terminology with local usage. For example, when we work with districts to localize these surveys we replace "principal supervisor" with the actual title in the district. Principals attend many meetings with other principals throughout the year so we also insert the specific title of the principals meetings that principal supervisors facilitate.
- *Timing.* We validated the surveys from which these items come as year-end surveys and the wording of many items assumes that time frame. Districts that want to use these items in surveys administered earlier in the year should consider adapting the items accordingly. We also encourage districts to survey their principals and principal supervisors annually, thereby allowing for year over year comparisons important to understanding professional growth.

Principal Survey Items

Rating scales. Unless noted below, items require a five-point agreement scale (i.e., Strongly agree, Disagree, Neutral, Agree, Strongly agree).

SECTION 1: PRINCIPAL SUPERVISORS' ONE-ON-ONE WORK WITH PRINCIPALS

Helped principals lead their own learning

Thinking about the past school year, to what extent do you agree or disagree with the following statements about your one-on-one work with your principal supervisor:

- My principal supervisor helped me develop a plan to lead my own learning as an instructional leader.
- My principal supervisor helped me access resources so I could lead my own learning as an instructional leader.
- My principal supervisor worked with me on my plan to lead my own learning as an instructional leader.
- The district's principal evaluation process helped me grow as an instructional leader.
- My principal supervisor used the district's principal evaluation process to help me grow as an instructional leader.

Teaching-and-learning moves: Joint work

- During the past school year, approximately how many times per month did your principal supervisor visit your school? [Response: numerical scale]

Thinking about the past school year, to what extent do you agree or disagree with the following statements about your one-on-one work with your principal supervisor:

- My principal supervisor and I set shared goals together.
- My principal supervisor and I learned together.

- My principal supervisor demonstrated that their main priority is my growth as an instructional leader.
- My principal supervisor and I spent almost all of our time together on my growth as an instructional leader.
- My principal supervisor valued my growth as an instructional leader.
- My principal supervisor helped me value my own growth as an instructional leader.
- My principal supervisor and I agreed on our definition of instructional leadership.

Teaching-and-learning moves: Modeling

- When working with you one-on-one during the past school year, how frequently did your principal supervisor use modeling to help you grow as an instructional leader? [Response: 5-point frequency scale]
- When working with you one-on-one during the past school year, how frequently did your principal supervisor model how to engage in the following instructional leadership activities? [Response: 5-point frequency scale]
  - Observing the quality of teaching in classrooms
  - Providing feedback to teachers to improve their teaching
  - Leading teacher professional development
  - Leading school improvement planning processes
  - Analyzing data/evidence for school improvement
  - Developing teacher leadership
- Overall, when working with you one-on-one during the past school year, how effective was your principal supervisor's use of modeling to help you grow as an instructional leader? [Response: 5-point effectiveness scale]

Teaching-and-learning moves: Talk

- When working with you one-on-one during the past school year, how frequently did your principal supervisor use talk moves[6] to help you grow as an instructional leader? [Response: 5-point frequency scale]

- When working with you one-on-one during the past school year, how frequently did your principal supervisor use talk moves to help you engage in the following instructional leadership activities? [Response: 5-point frequency scale]
  - Observing the quality of teaching in classrooms
  - Providing feedback to teachers to improve their teaching
  - Leading teacher professional development
  - Leading school improvement planning processes
  - Analyzing data/evidence for school improvement
  - Developing teacher leadership
- Overall, when working with you one-on-one during the past school year, how effective was your principal supervisor's use of talk moves to help you grow as an instructional leader? [Response: 5-point effectiveness scale]

Teaching-and-learning moves: Differentiation

- When working with you one-on-one during the past school year, how frequently did your principal supervisor differentiate their support to help you grow as an instructional leader? [Response: 5-point frequency scale]
- When working with you one-on-one during the past school year, how frequently did your principal supervisor differentiate their support to help you engage in the following instructional leadership activities? [Response: 5-point frequency scale]
  - Observing the quality of teaching in classrooms
  - Providing feedback to teachers to improve their teaching
  - Leading teacher professional development
  - Leading school improvement planning processes
  - Analyzing data/evidence for school improvement
  - Developing teacher leadership
- Overall, when working with you one-on-one during the past school year, how effective was your principal supervisor's use

of differentiation to help you grow as an instructional leader? [Response: 5-point effectiveness scale]

Thinking about the past school year, to what extent do you agree or disagree with the following statements about your one-on-one work with your principal supervisor:

- My principal supervisor knew my strengths as an instructional leader.
- My principal supervisor knew my areas for growth as an instructional leader.
- My principal supervisor made decisions about how to support me based on my strengths as an instructional leader.
- My principal supervisor made decisions about how to support me based on my areas for growth as an instructional leader.

Teaching-and-learning moves: Brokering

- When working with you one-on-one during the past school year, how frequently did your principal supervisor connect you to outside resources to help you grow as an instructional leader? [Response: 5-point frequency scale]
- When working with you one-on-one during the past school year, how frequently did your principal supervisor connect you to outside resources to help you engage with the following instructional leadership activities? [Response: 5-point frequency scale]
  - Observing the quality of teaching in classrooms
  - Providing feedback to teachers to improve their teaching
  - Leading teacher professional development
  - Leading school improvement planning processes
  - Analyzing data/evidence for school improvement
  - Developing teacher leadership
- Overall, when working with you one-on-one during the past school year, how effective were those outside resources to help you grow as an instructional leader? [Response: 5-point effectiveness scale]

- When working with you one-on-one during the past school year, how frequently did your principal supervisor protect your time to help you grow as an instructional leader? [Response: 5-point frequency scale]
- When working with you one-on-one during the past school year, how frequently did your principal supervisor protect your time to engage in the following instructional leadership activities? [Response: 5-point frequency scale]
  - Observing the quality of teaching in classrooms
  - Providing feedback to teachers to improve their teaching
  - Leading teacher professional development
  - Leading school improvement planning processes
  - Analyzing data/evidence for school improvement
  - Developing teacher leadership
- Overall, when working with you one-on-one during the past school year, how effectively did your principal supervisor protect your time to help you grow as an instructional leader? [Response: 5-point effectiveness scale]

SECTION 2: PRINCIPAL SUPERVISORS' LEADERSHIP OF PRINCIPALS MEETINGS

Authentic tasks in a scope-and-sequence

Thinking about your principals meetings during the past school year, to what extent do you agree or disagree with the following statements:

- My principal supervisor organized our meeting activities to support my growth as an instructional leader.
- The activities in our principals meetings supplemented my own learning plan.
- We spent the majority of our time in principals meetings focused on real instructional leadership work in real time.
- My principal supervisor organized our meeting activities in a logical sequence across the year.
- The activities in our principals meetings became progressively more challenging over the course of the year.

Teaching-and-learning moves: Joint work

- During the past school year, approximately how many principals meetings did you attend? [Response: numerical scale]

Thinking about your principals meetings during the past school year, to what extent do you agree or disagree with the following statements:

- My principal supervisor always facilitated my principals meetings.
- My principals meetings always took place at a school site.
- My principal supervisor demonstrated during meetings that principals' growth as instructional leaders was a priority for them.
- My principal supervisor, other principals, and I set shared meeting goals together.
- The work we did during meetings helped me value my growth as an instructional leader.
- We spent almost all of our meeting time focused on helping principals grow as instructional leaders.
- I was fully engaged in meeting activities.
- We worked on topics important to me.
- I planned part of a meeting.
- I led part of a meeting.

Teaching-and-learning moves: Modeling

- During the past school year's principals meetings, how frequently did your principal supervisor use modeling to help you grow as an instructional leader? [Response: 5-point frequency scale]
- During the past school year's principals meetings, how frequently did your principal supervisor model how to engage in the following instructional leadership activities? [Response: 5-point frequency scale]
  - Observing the quality of teaching in classrooms
  - Providing feedback to teachers to improve their teaching

- Leading teacher professional development
- Leading school improvement planning processes
- Analyzing data/evidence for school improvement
- Developing teacher leadership

- Overall, during the past school year's principals meetings, how effective was your principal supervisor's use of modeling to help you grow as an instructional leader? [Response: 5-point effectiveness scale]

Teaching-and-learning moves: Talk moves

- During the past school year's principals meetings, how frequently did your principal supervisor use talk moves to help you grow as an instructional leader? [Response: 5-point frequency scale]
- During the past school year's principals meetings, how frequently did your principal supervisor use talk moves to help you engage with the following instructional leadership activities? [Response: 5-point frequency scale]
  - Observing the quality of teaching in classrooms
  - Providing feedback to teachers to improve their teaching
  - Leading teacher professional development
  - Leading school improvement planning processes
  - Analyzing data/evidence for school improvement
  - Developing teacher leadership
- Overall, during the past school year's principals meetings, how effective was your principal supervisor's use of talk moves to help you grow as an instructional leader? [Response: 5-point effectiveness scale]

Teaching-and-learning moves: Differentiation

- During the past school year's principals meetings, how frequently did your principal supervisor differentiate their support to help you grow as an instructional leader? [Response: 5-point frequency scale]
- During the past school year's principals meetings, how frequently did your principal supervisor differentiate their support

to you to help you engage in the following instructional leadership activities during principals meetings? [Response: 5-point frequency scale]
  - Observing the quality of teaching in classrooms
  - Providing feedback to teachers to improve their teaching
  - Leading teacher professional development
  - Leading school improvement planning processes
  - Analyzing data/evidence for school improvement
  - Developing teacher leadership
- Overall, during the past school year's principals meetings, how effective was your principal supervisor's use of differentiation to help you grow as an instructional leader? [Response: 5-point effectiveness scale]

Thinking about your principals meetings during the past school year, to what extent do you agree or disagree with the following statements about your work with your principal supervisor:

- My principal supervisor led activities tailored to my strengths as an instructional leader.
- My principal supervisors led activities tailored to my areas for growth as an instructional leader.

Teaching-and-learning moves: Brokering

- During the past school year's principals meetings, how frequently did your principal supervisor connect you to outside resources to help you grow as an instructional leader? [Response: 5-point frequency scale]
- During the past school year's principals meetings, how frequently did your principal supervisor connect you to outside resources to help you engage in the following instructional leadership activities? [Response: 5-point frequency scale]
  - Observing the quality of teaching in classrooms
  - Providing feedback to teachers to improve their teaching
  - Leading teacher professional development
  - Leading school improvement planning processes

  - Analyzing data/evidence for school improvement
  - Developing teacher leadership
- Overall, during the past school year's principals meetings, how effective were those outside resources to help you grow as an instructional leader? [Response: 5-point effectiveness scale]
- During the past school year's principals meetings, how frequently did your principal supervisor protect your time to help you grow as an instructional leader? [Response: 5-point frequency scale]
- During the past school year's principals meetings, how frequently did your principal supervisor protect your time to engage in the following instructional leadership activities? [Response: 5-point frequency scale]
  - Observing the quality of teaching in classrooms
  - Providing feedback to teachers to improve their teaching
  - Leading teacher professional development
  - Leading school improvement planning processes
  - Analyzing data/evidence for school improvement
  - Developing teacher leadership
- Overall, during the past school year's principals meetings, how effectively did your principal supervisor protect your time to help you grow as an instructional leader? [Response: 5-point effectiveness scale]

Teaching-and-learning moves: Identifying all principals as learning resources

Thinking about your principals meetings during the past school year, to what extent do you agree or disagree with the following statements:

- My principal supervisor provided time for me to teach other principals to help us grow as instructional leaders.
- My principal supervisor provided time for me to give feedback to other principals to help us grow as instructional leaders.
- My principal supervisor highlighted my strengths as an instructional leader.

- My principal supervisor organized me and other principals into small groups in ways that helped me grow as an instructional leader.
- My principal connected me with other principals as learning resources to help us grow as instructional leaders.

SECTION 3: OUTCOMES

- During an average week of the past school year, approximately what percentage of your work time did you spend on activities related to instructional leadership? [Response: numerical scale]
- What percentage of your work time do you believe you should spend on activities related to instructional leadership? [Response: numerical scale]
- Thinking about your leadership over the course of the past school year, how would you rate the improvement in the quality of your work as an instructional leader? [Response: 5-point amount scale]
- Thinking about your leadership today, how would you rate the overall quality of your instructional leadership? [Response: 5-point quality scale]
- Thinking about your leadership today, how would you rate the quality of your work in the following instructional leadership activities [Response: 5-point quality scale]
  - Observing the quality of teaching in classrooms
  - Providing feedback to teachers to improve their teaching
  - Leading teacher professional development
  - Leading school improvement planning processes
  - Analyzing data/evidence for school improvement
  - Developing teacher leadership
- Thinking about the past school year overall, how effective or not effective to your development in the following areas was your one-on-one work with your principal supervisor? [Response: 5-point amount scale]
  - Observing the quality of teaching in classrooms
  - Providing feedback to teachers to improve their teaching
  - Leading teacher professional development

  - Leading school improvement planning processes
  - Analyzing data/evidence for school improvement
  - Developing teacher leadership
- Thinking about the past school year overall, how effective or not effective to your development in the following areas was your work with your principal supervisor in principals meetings? [Response: 5-point amount scale]
  - Observing the quality of teaching in classrooms
  - Providing feedback to teachers to improve their teaching
  - Leading teacher professional development
  - Leading school improvement planning processes
  - Analyzing data/evidence for school improvement
  - Developing teacher leadership

PRINCIPAL SUPERVISOR SURVEY ITEMS

Sections 1-3: One-on-one work, principals meetings, and outcomes

For Sections 1-3, adapt the items you use in your principals' survey to elicit principal supervisors' perspectives on the same items. The following provides one example of such an adaptation of the one-on-one modeling items:

- When working with ~~you~~ your principals one-on-one during the past school year, how frequently did ~~your principal supervisor~~ you use modeling to help ~~you~~ your principals grow as ~~an~~ instructional leaders?
- When working with ~~you~~ your principals one-on-one during the past school year, how frequently did ~~your principal supervisor~~ you model how to engage in the following instructional leadership activities?
  - Observing the quality of teaching in classrooms
  - Providing feedback to teachers to improve their teaching
  - Leading teacher professional development
  - Leading school improvement planning processes
  - Analyzing data/evidence for school improvement
  - Developing teacher leadership

- Overall, when working with ~~you~~ your principals one-on-one during the past school year, how effective was ~~your principal supervisor~~ your use of modeling to help ~~you~~ your principals grow as ~~an~~ instructional leaders?

SECTION 4: ITEMS ON THE SUPPORTS FOR PRINCIPAL SUPERVISORS WORK WITH PRINCIPALS

Rating scales. Unless noted below, items require a five-point agreement scale (i.e., Strongly agree, Disagree, Neutral, Agree, Strongly agree).

Principal role definition

Thinking about the past school year, to what extent do you agree or disagree with the following statements about your principals:

- All of my principals understood that their main job was instructional leadership.
- All of my principals saw themselves as instructional leaders.
- All of my principals and I agreed on our definition of instructional leadership.
- The district's formal job description for principals emphasized that their main job was instructional leadership.
- The district's formal evaluation system for principals emphasized that their main job was instructional leadership.
- The district's hiring and selection process for principals screened for strong instructional leaders.
- The superintendent or other executive staff communicated to principals that their main job was instructional leadership.
- Staff throughout the central office understood that the main job of principals was instructional leadership.

Principal supervisor role definition

Thinking about the past school year, to what extent do you agree or disagree with the following statements about your role as principal supervisor:

- My primary responsibility was to support principals' growth as instructional leaders.
- My formal job description emphasized that my main job was to support principals' growth as instructional leaders.
- The superintendent and other executive staff communicated to me that my main job was to support principals' growth as instructional leaders.
- The superintendent and other executive staff communicated throughout the district that my main job was to support principals' growth as instructional leaders.
- My principals understood that my main job was to support their growth as instructional leaders.
- Other central office staff understood that my main job was to support principals' growth as instructional leaders.
- My principals asked me to help them with matters related to instructional leadership.
- My principals asked me to help them with matters related to school operations.
- Other central office staff took my time away from supporting principals' growth as instructional leaders.

Positional authority

Thinking about the past school year, to what extent do you agree or disagree with the following statements about your role as principal supervisor:

- I had the financial resources I needed to support my principals' growth as instructional leaders.
- I had the staff I needed to support my principals' growth as instructional leaders.
- I had the autonomy I needed to support my principals' growth as instructional leaders.
- I had the authority I needed to support my principals' growth as instructional leaders.
- I had help from other principal supervisors to support my principals' growth as instructional leaders.

- I had help from other central office staff to support my principals' growth as instructional leaders.
- I had the data I needed to make evidence-based decisions about how to support my principals' growth as instructional leaders.

Organization of principals

- During the past school year, how many principals were assigned to you? [Response: numerical scale]
- How many of the principals assigned to you did you work with for the first time starting in the past school year? [Response: numerical scale]
- How many of the principals assigned to you were first-year principals during the past school year? [Response: numerical scale]

Thinking about the past school year, to what extent do you agree or disagree with the following statements about your principals:

- I was responsible for the right number of principals.
- I had enough time to meet with all of my principals as often as I felt necessary.
- A small number of principals took up most of my time.
- I had the right skill set to help my principals grow as instructional leaders.
- The composition of my principals helped me help my principals grow as instructional leaders.

Hiring

Thinking about the past school year, to what extent do you agree or disagree with the following statements about your role as principal supervisor:

- The district's formal job description for principal supervisors emphasized that my main job was to help principals grow as instructional leaders.
- The district's hiring and selection process for principal supervisors screened for strong capacity to help principals grow as instructional leaders.

- My principal supervisor colleagues view their main role as helping principals grow as instructional leaders.
- My principal supervisor colleagues take responsibility for leading their own learning.

Professional learning

- Did you work with an outside coach? [Response: Yes/No]

If yes, to what extent do you agree or disagree with the following statements about your work with the outside coach? If no, skip to the questions about support for your professional growth below.

- I had the help from my outside coach that I needed to help me improve how I support my principals' growth as instructional leaders.
- I spent the right amount of time with my coach to help me improve how I support my principals' growth as instructional leaders.
- My coach helped me lead my own learning in how I support principals' growth as instructional leaders.
- My coach supplemented my efforts to lead my own learning in ways important to my professional growth.
- My coach modeled for me how to support principals' growth as instructional leaders when working with principals one-on-one.
- My coach used talk moves in ways that helped me support principals' growth as instructional leaders when working with principals one-on-one.
- My coach differentiated their support to me in ways that helped me support principals' growth as instructional leaders when working with principals one-on-one.
- My coach connected me with the rest of the central office in ways that helped me support principals' growth as instructional leaders when working with principals one-on-one.
- My coach buffered me from the rest of the central office in ways that helped me support principals' growth as instructional leaders when working with principals one-on-one.

- My coach took my time away from supporting principals' growth as instructional leaders one-on-one.
- Overall, how effectively did your coach support you in how you take a teaching-and-learning approach when working with principals one-on-one?
- My coach modeled for me how to support principals' growth as instructional leaders when working in principals meetings.
- My coach used talk moves in ways that helped me support principals' growth as instructional leaders when working in principals meetings.
- My coach differentiated their support to me in ways that helped me support principals' growth as instructional leaders when working in principals meetings.
- My coach connected me with the rest of the central office in ways that helped me support principals' growth as instructional leaders when working in principals meetings.
- My coach buffered me from the rest of the central office in ways that helped me support principals' growth as instructional leaders when working in principals meetings.
- My coach took my time away from supporting principals' growth as instructional leaders when working in principals meetings.
- Overall, how effectively did your coach support you in how you take a teaching-and-learning approach when working in principals meetings?

Thinking about the past school year, to what extent do you agree or disagree with the following statements about support for your professional growth?

- I led my own learning.
- I worked with my principal supervisor colleagues to support our professional growth.
- I protected my own time to support my work with principals on their growth as instructional leaders.

- My principal supervisor colleagues and I worked together to protect our time to work with principals on their growth as instructional leaders.

Supervisor of Principal Supervisors

Thinking about the past school year, to what extent do you agree or disagree with the following statements about your supervisor:

- I had the help from my supervisor I needed to help me grow in my ability to support my principals' growth as instructional leaders when working with them one-on-one.
- My supervisor valued my growth in my ability to support principals' growth as instructional leaders when working with them one-on-one.
- My supervisor helped me lead my own learning in how to support principals' growth as instructional leaders.
- My supervisor dedicated sufficient time to supporting my professional growth.
- My supervisor modeled for me how to support principals' growth as instructional leaders when working with principals one-on-one.
- My supervisor used talk moves in ways that helped me support principals' growth as instructional leaders when working with principals one-on-one.
- My supervisor differentiated their support to me in ways that helped me support principals' growth as instructional leaders when working with principals one-on-one.
- My supervisor connected me with the rest of the central office in ways that helped me support principals' growth as instructional leaders when working with principals one-on-one.
- My supervisor buffered me from the rest of the central office in ways that helped me support principals' growth as instructional leaders when working with principals one-on-one.
- My supervisor took my time away from supporting principals' growth as instructional leaders one-on-one.

- Overall, how effectively did your supervisor support you in how you take a teaching-and-learning approach when working with principals one-on-one?
- My supervisor modeled for me how to support principals' growth as instructional leaders when working in principals meetings.
- My supervisor used talk moves in ways that helped me support principals' growth as instructional leaders when working in principals meetings.
- My supervisor differentiated their support to me in ways that helped me support principals' growth as instructional leaders when working in principals meetings.
- My supervisor connected me with the rest of the central office in ways that helped me support principals' growth as instructional leaders when working in principals meetings.
- My supervisor buffered me from the rest of the central office in ways that helped me support principals' growth as instructional leaders when working in principals meetings.
- My supervisor took my time away from supporting principals' growth as instructional leaders when working in principals meetings.
- Overall, how effectively did your supervisor support you in how you take a teaching-and-learning approach when working in principals meetings?

Progress with central office transformation

Thinking about the past school year, to what extent do you agree or disagree that central office staff in the following areas worked in ways that helped you support principals' growth as instructional leaders:

- Curriculum and Instruction/Teaching and Learning/Academics
- Human Resources
- Budget/Finance
- Facilities/Maintenance

- Research/Evaluation/Assessment
- Student Services/Special Services (e.g. Special Education)
- Family and Community Engagement
- Technology
- Nutrition Services
- Safety/Security

Thinking about the past school year, to what extent do you agree or disagree that central office staff in the following areas worked effectively to support principals:

- Curriculum and Instruction/Teaching and Learning/Academics
- Human Resources
- Budget/Finance
- Facilities/Maintenance
- Research/Evaluation/Assessment
- Student Services/Special Services (e.g. Special Education)
- Family and Community Engagement
- Technology
- Nutrition Services
- Safety/Security

EXHIBIT 3

Professional Growth Planning Process

This professional growth planning process (PGPP) engages principal supervisors in leading their own learning toward their own and their districts' performance goals. Our approach builds on research on adult learning that shows professionals improve their practice when they lead their own growth as a regular part of their daily work.

But district professional development at best tends to *get done to* professionals rather than fostering professionals' agency over their own learning day-to-day in real settings. As a classroom teacher and principal, you were probably pulled out of your school for workshops developed and run by the central office. Union contracts likely designated specific time for your professional learning. Your district may have required you to submit goals for the year, but not to actually use them to develop and implement plans for realizing them. You received your evaluation results at the end of the year as a summary assessment rather than guide for your work. But now in your principal supervisory role, research and experience suggest you have to pivot away from such relative passive learning and toward active leadership of your own learning. Where to begin?

This PGPP suggests activities you can use to lead your own learning. You may also want to adapt this tool to help your principals lead their own learning. This tool stems from our own and others' research underscoring the importance of a *cycle of inquiry* approach that prompts you to: self-assess, develop a learning plan, plan to track your progress, take action, and reassess and begin again (see figure E3.1). We elaborate on each of these parts in the following five sections. Throughout this discussion, we prompt you to use these ideas as jumping-off points to design a process that you understand and own.

FIGURE E3.1 The cycle of inquiry

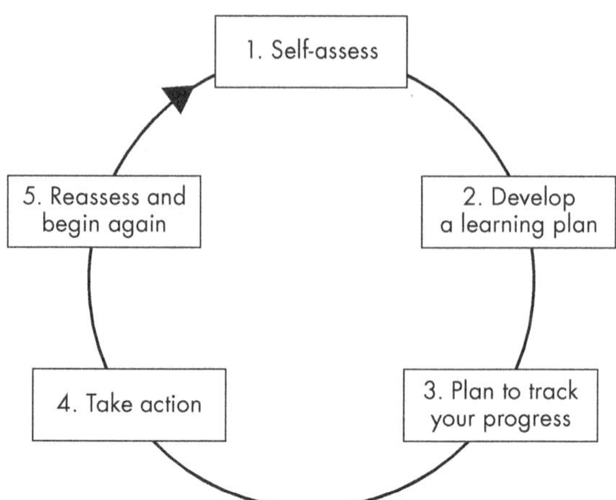

1: SELF-ASSESS

First, work with evidence to assess how close your current practice is with the ways of working to which you aspire. Such self-assessments can help you see yourself on a pathway to reaching your goals—which is important to your actually progressing toward them—and identify meaningful plans for improvement. By the end of this part, you will have a completed evidence-based self-assessment to guide your development of a learning plan. Figure E3.2 outlines the processes in this part.

Get Organized for Self-Assessment

Before you start, decide which standards you will use from the principal supervisor performance standards (exhibit 1) to anchor your self-assessment. Then, integrate the standards into an organizer for capturing your work, using a rubric indicating the depth of implementation of each standard. Table E3.1 provides one example.

FIGURE E3.2 Self-assessment process

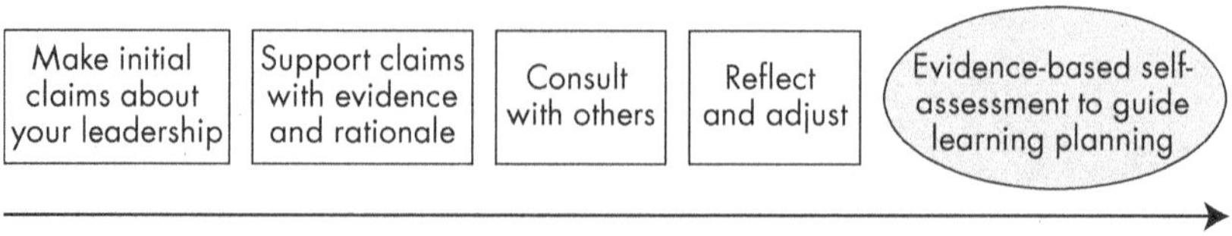

Make initial claims about your leadership	Support claims with evidence and rationale	Consult with others	Reflect and adjust	Evidence-based self-assessment to guide learning planning

TABLE E3.1 Self-assessment along your professional standards

	CLAIMS				
	NOT ADOPTING Does not yet talk about their practice or engage in practices consistent with the standard.	ADOPTING THE TALK Talks about their practice in ways consistent with the standard, but actual practice does not yet reflect the standard.	ENGAGING AT A SURFACE LEVEL Practice begins to reflect the standard, but does not yet demonstrate deep understanding of which practices are consistent with the standard or why to engage in those practices.	ENGAGING WITH UNDERSTANDING (1) Practice often reflects the standard and demonstrates deepening understanding of what practices are consistent with the standard and why to engage in those practices. (2) Practices consistent with the standard are a regular part of daily practice.	MASTERY (1) Practice routinely reflects the standard at the level of "engaging with understanding" across multiple contexts and years. (2) Practice across settings and over time demonstrates the ability to improvise—to use the standard as a jumping-off point to develop new ways of working consistent with the standard and likely to contribute to progressively more powerful results.
Standard 1 [write in]					
Evidence					
Rationale					
Standard 2 [write in]					
Evidence					
Rationale					
. . .					

Make Initial Claims, and Support Them with Evidence and Rationale

As prompted in table E3.1, for your self-assessment, make claims about your leadership along each standard and check your claim with evidence and an explicit rationale.

- *Claim: A clear, measurable statement about the quality of your current ability to lead along each standard.* When we make claims, rather than rely on numbers (e.g., "On Standard 4, I am a 3"), we literally describe ourselves in relation to each standard—an approach that improves the accuracy of our ratings. Scales such as those that proceed from "Basic" to "Proficient" do not always describe true markers of how people learn, so pay special attention to the measurability and validity of your scale.
- *Evidence: Concrete examples and other data that illustrate how you lead along each standard.* Evidence should make your leadership visible in ways that help you check the accuracy of your claim and provide a baseline for assessing your growth over time. Think broadly about what counts as true evidence of your leadership; this generally will not include school test scores but rather data from principal survey results, emails to and from principals, and notes from observations of your work with principals. Do the best with the data you have and plan to collect progressively better data each year. Table E3.2 provides some guidance on distinguishing strong from weak evidence of *your own practice.*
- *Rationale: Your explanation for why you think your evidence supports your claim.* When we pause to articulate our rationales, we make our thinking visible to ourselves and others, increasing the accuracy of our self-assessments and deepening our reflections. Writing down your evidence and rationales also creates a record of your thinking to which you can refer to over time.

As an example of this process, one principal supervisor assessing herself on the DL2 principal supervisor performance standards wrote the responses shown in table E3.3.

TABLE E3.2 Strong versus weak evidence

STRONG EVIDENCE	WEAK EVIDENCE
Describes *how* you lead	Identifies activities in which you participated without describing how you led in those activities in relation to given standards
Specifically supports the claim you are making about the quality of your leadership along specific standards	Talks about your leadership without illustrating how your leadership reflects your claim about the quality of your leadership along specific standards
For claims that suggest frequency of action across contexts, provides multiple examples across contexts	Provides single examples
For claims about level of understanding, includes descriptions showing your understanding related to the specific standard	Does not indicate how you understand the standard and your practice in relation to the standard

TABLE E3.3 Same self-assessment responses

Standard 1: Dedicates their time to helping principals grow as instructional leaders

CLAIM: ADOPTING THE TALK
I talk about my leadership practice in ways consistent with dedicating my time to helping principals grow as instructional leaders but my actual practice does not yet reflect that I actually dedicate the majority of my time in this way.
Evidence My colleagues have observed me telling principals that my job is to focus as much of my time as possible on their instructional leadership. For instance, my supervisor's scripted notes at the January 6th meeting shows I said, "I'm in this with you. While you are maximizing your time with teachers, I am maximizing my time with you." But a review of my calendar shows that between January and May, I spent only about 35 percent of my time in a given week working directly with principals. For example, the week of February 6th I spent about two hours each in 4 schools and otherwise was in central office and community meetings related to school staffing, high school reform, school boundaries, and parent complaints.

continued

TABLE E3.3 *continued*

Rationale
I have had my assistant edit my calendar so it reflects how I actually spend my time rather than how I planned to spend my time, so it provides solid evidence of the amount of time I actually spent with principals as well as the limited extent to which my other tasks were in direct enough support of principals' growth as instructional leaders. For instance, sometimes when I work on staffing, that work is to ensure principals do not lose time on instruction. But in most of the cases on my calendar during that period, I was working on more general staffing issues or doing staffing tasks for principals instead of teaching them how to do them.

Consult with Others

Sharing your work with others for feedback can increase your understanding of the standards, your claims, and your evidence as well as the accuracy of your ratings. Here is one suggested protocol for this process:

1. Choose one claim-evidence-rationale set and give your partner time to review your work.
2. Pose questions to solicit their critical feedback, such as:
   - What clarifying questions do you have about this claim-evidence-rationale set?
   - How well does my evidence help you see the quality of my leadership?
   - How well does my evidence actually support the claim I am making?
   - How well does my rationale explain why I think my evidence supports my claim?
   - Anything else?
3. Switch roles with your partner.
4. Repeat.
5. Use the feedback to improve your self-assessment.

2: DEVELOP A LEARNING PLAN

This part guides you in moving from learning goals to developing an actual plan for realizing those goals. You will base your learning

FIGURE E3.3 Process for developing a learning plan

Choose focus standards → Identify resources and opportunities → Set growth targets → Reflect, adjust, and schedule calendar →

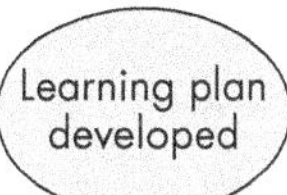

plan on research showing that adults learn to deepen their practice not mainly through formal learning opportunities like conferences or workshops but by accessing learning supports while doing their daily work. By the end of this step, you will have an intentional learning plan likely to help you realize your growth targets. Figure E3.3 outlines the processes in this step.

Get Organized to Develop a Learning Plan

First, develop a template for representing your learning plan. Table E3.4 provides one suggestion with the basic elements that help you interrogate and strengthen your own choices about what to include in your plan.

TABLE E3.4 Learning plan

SELF-ASSESSMENT	RESOURCES AND OPPORTUNITIES	GROWTH GOALS	RATIONALE
I am starting at this level of leadership capacity related to my focus standards.	And if I utilize these learning resources and opportunities in these particular ways . . .	. . . then I will be able to make this claim about my leadership along my focus standards by the spring.	And I think so because . . .

Choose Focus Standards

All the leadership performance standards you are using are no doubt important aspects of your leadership, but addressing them all likely will stretch you too thin. Research on the development of expertise shows that adults grow in multiple areas by going deep in a few and transferring that learning to other areas. So choose two or three standards as your focus for this year and, in later years, gradually add more standards. In the process, focus on standards on which you rated yourself relatively high. Focusing on your strengths increases your motivation to learn and gives you a chance to become familiar with the professional growth process before tackling your more challenging standards. If you are using table E3.4, enter the claims about your leadership along with your focus standards in the first column.

Identify Learning Resources and Opportunities

Now, identify the *learning resources and opportunities* that will help you grow along your focus standards this year. As you do, remember that various research on adult learning shows that formal settings outside our regular work, like professional conferences and workshops at the central office, are among the least supportive forms of professional growth especially compared to those we access as we go about our daily routine.

Remember, too, that the question here is not: What next leadership actions will I take that relate to a given standard? Rather, ask yourself: *What will I do next to support my learning along each of my focus standards?* Especially experienced leaders tend to assume that simply by performing certain leadership actions (e.g., providing coaching, running a meeting) they will grow in the process. We do improve our leadership as we go about our daily work, but when we do so *in certain ways*—for example, when you receive feedback or coaching as you work or document how you perform a particular task and deeply reflect on what you did.

Link Learning Resources and Opportunities to Your Focus Standards

Next, use the results of your brainstorming to begin aligning particular learning resources and opportunities to each focus standard, using the Resource and Opportunity Map (ROMp) shown in table E3.5 or some other organizer. Remember that the same learning resource or opportunity could help you grow along multiple standards, so you don't necessarily need an entirely new set of resources and opportunities for each standard. Do try to distinguish *how* you will need to engage with each resource or opportunity to support your growth on a particular standard. In the process, avoid shorthand, which could suggest you are not thinking deeply enough about your learning plan and may be hard for you to decipher later.

For example, you may plan to attend a conference, but which specific sessions? How will you network with particular people as learning resources? Spell out those details of your participation in your plan. Articulating your rationale—why you think a particular learning support may be helpful—is one way to check that you have described each resource and opportunity at a sufficient level of detail.

TABLE E3.5 Resources and Opportunities Map (ROMp) example

Focus Standard 1: Support the learning of other adults through a teaching and learning stance in ways that increase equitable learning for each student.

LIST	DETAIL	EXPLAIN
Book, Everyday Antiracism	Get on agenda of principal supervisor meeting for group book talk that I facilitate. Get feedback on facilitation plan from Michael. During meeting, have Kim take notes of my moves and participants' engagement. Debrief with participants. Review notes and discuss with Michael.	If I first practice facilitating this book talk with my colleagues, then I will receive important practice and feedback to strengthen how I do it with my principals from a teaching and learning stance.

continued

TABLE E3.5 *continued*

LIST	DETAIL	EXPLAIN
Michael	Schedule him to observe me facilitating the book talk including time to debrief. Schedule two opportunities for him to shadow me during one-on-one visits with principals and for real-time coaching and feedback.	Michael will be honest with me about how well I am doing. He also provides better feedback when he takes notes, so I will specifically prompt him to do that.

Once you've mapped out your learning resources and opportunities, make sure you've captured your thinking in your learning plan from table E3.4 or whatever organizer you are using.

Set Growth Targets

If you access those resources and opportunities, how far do you think you can grow along each standard? One whole level? Part or most of the way toward that level? Use questions like those to set ambitious but realistic growth targets. Checking your rationale can help you ensure you identify the right targets. Use table E3.4 or your other organizer to capture your drafts and your initial full learning plan.

Consult with Others

Feedback at this point may be especially helpful to ensuring that you: (1) specify the learning resources and opportunities you will access, and (2) emphasize learning on the job. The following protocol may be useful for this purpose:

1. Choose your plan for growth along one standard and give your partner a chance to review.
2. Pose questions such as:
   - What clarifying questions do you have about what my plan involves?
   - How well have I specified what I will do when?

   - To what extent does my learning plan emphasize learning on the job?
   - Other resources and opportunities I might consider? Ones to reconsider or omit?
   - How well does my rationale explain why I think my specific plans will help me grow along that standard? Suggestions for improvement?
   - Anything else?
3. Switch roles with your partner.
4. Repeat for your other focus standard(s).
5. Use the feedback to improve your learning plan.

Reflect, Adjust, and Schedule Your Calendar Accordingly

Move the tasks in your learning plan into your work calendar. For example, remember that feedback you wanted to get from your colleagues? When will you connect with them before the observation to brief them on what would be helpful? Is the session they will observe on their calendars? Have you blocked off time to prepare for the session? When will you debrief? If you have someone who helps you with your calendar, consider asking them to schedule meetings and work time based on your learning plan.

3: PLAN TO TRACK YOUR PROGRESS

In this part, you will plan to assess progress before you take action on your learning plan to help ensure that you are collecting the data you need all along the way to make midcourse corrections and understand your growth toward your leadership targets over time. Chances are your district's data system will not provide the data you need to understand your progress. Be sure to take full advantage of available data, but definitely plan to collect new data yourself. By the end of this part, you will have a plan to assess the extent to which you have implemented your learning plan, grown in your own leadership, and supported principals' growth as instructional leaders. Figure E3.4 outlines the processes in this part.

FIGURE E3.4 Process for tracking your progress

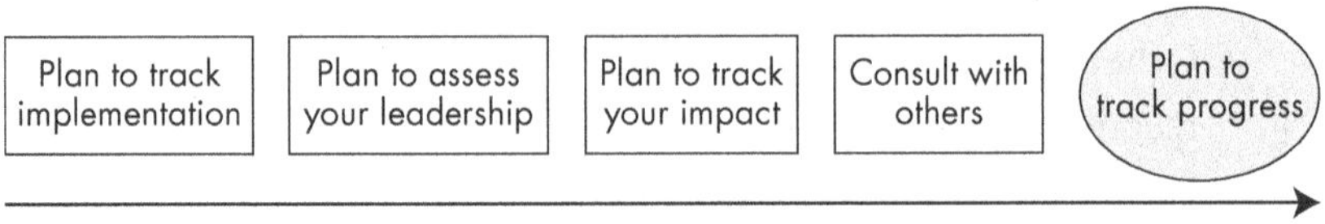

Plan to track implementation	Plan to assess your leadership	Plan to track your impact	Consult with others	Plan to track progress

Get Organized to Plan to Track Your Progress

First, develop templates for capturing your plan to track your progress. Throughout this part we provide some examples. However you choose to proceed, make sure your templates prompt you to spell out the following basic components of a plan to assess progress:

- *Measures.* What you would see happening if implementation were occurring at a particular level.
- *Data collection activities.* How you will capture information to determine if those things are happening.

Plan to Track Learning Plan Implementation

To what extent am I doing what I said I would do in my learning plan? Completely? Well? Sometimes we do not realize our growth goals, not because we did not develop the right plan, but because we did not fully implement it. Tracking the quality of your plan's implementation can help you make that distinction. Table E3.6 prompts you to include the basic features of a plan to assess implementation and provides an example.

Plan to Assess Your Leadership

How have I led along each standard? Too often, leaders lack the basic evidence they need to understand their growth because they do not collect the right evidence along the way. Plan to identify and track meaningful measures and evidence of your growth along your focus standards. In the process, remember that data about your leadership is just that—information about moves you make day-to-day. Take care not to confuse this with data about how teachers or other adults work, which is information about their practice and, possibly, the impact of your leadership (which you will plan to track in the next sec-

TABLE E3.6 Plan to assess implementation of your learning plan

LEARNING RESOURCES AND OPPORTUNITIES (FROM STEP 2)	MEASURES	DATA COLLECTION ACTIVITIES
If I utilize these learning resources and opportunities . . .	. . . which I will know I am using because I will see this concrete evidence in practice . . .	. . . which I will collect in the following ways
Michael observing me lead the book study meeting.	Meetings and debrief/feedback sessions occur. I have a set of observation notes from Michael. My notes from the debrief sessions indicate that Michael's feedback deepened my understanding of the quality of my leadership along this standard.	Have assistant color-code activities on my calendar as I complete them.

tion). Table E3.7 prompts you to include the basic features of a plan to assess your leadership and provides an example.

Plan to Track Your Impact

To what extent has my leadership had an impact on others that matters to results for students? Your influence on student learning is likely indirect, coming through your work with principals, which in turn should strengthen the quality of classroom teaching for each and every student. Plan to collect data mainly about your principals to help you understand your impact (see table E3.8). As you develop this plan, remember to be realistic. Many conditions besides your work with principals will affect their leadership. Ideally, in your work to differentiate supports for principals you are already collecting information on principal growth. Or, if principals are engaged in their own professional growth planning process, you can use the data they collect for this part of your process.

TABLE E3.7 Plan to assess your leadership

GROWTH GOALS (FROM STEP 2)	MEASURES	DATA COLLECTION ACTIVITIES
If I am progressing toward these growth goals . . .	. . . then I will see the following in my own practice . . .	. . . which I will document in the following ways.
Focus standard: My leadership practice in one-on-one meetings often reflects that I am leading the learning of principals in ways that will help them grow as instructional leaders and demonstrates that I understand what taking such a stance involves and why to take one.	Score above 3.5 on the DL2 Annual Survey of Principals on joint work, modeling, and tool use in one-on-one settings.	-Spring survey administration -Results provided to us before summer
Secondary standard: My leadership practice in my principals meetings often reflects that I am leading the learning of principals in ways that will help them grow as instructional leaders and demonstrates that I understand what such a stance involves and why to take one.	Score above 3.5 on the DL2 Annual Survey of Principals on joint work, modeling, and tool use in communities of practice meetings. Michael's observation notes consistently show me modeling for principals how to engage in instructional leadership. My lesson plans for my principals' meetings will contain differentiated prompts that are designed to support particular learning for each of my principals.	-Spring survey administration -Results provided to us before summer -Remind Michael to take notes and ask him to upload notes to shared OneNote folder. -Upload book study lesson plan to OneNote.

TABLE E3.8 Plan to assess impact

GROWTH GOALS	DIRECT IMPACT (ADULTS)	INDIRECT IMPACT (ADULTS)	ULTIMATE IMPACT (STUDENTS)
If realize these growth goals (from part 2) . . .	. . . then I am likely to see these changes in the adults I work with most directly . . .	. . . which in turn may lead to these changes in the practice of teachers (or other adults—in this case the principals my colleagues support) . . .	. . . which may contribute to the following improvements in student learning, especially those historically underserved by public schools.
My leadership practice in my principals meetings often reflects that I am learning of principals in ways that will help them grow as instructional leaders and demonstrates that I understand what such a stance involves and why to take one.	On the DL2 Annual Survey of Principals, at least 80% of my principals will report that they increased the amount of time they spend on instructional leadership tasks, that they have grown in their ability to engage in instructional leadership, and that the principals meetings I have facilitated have supported them with both.	The percentage of teachers my principals rate as proficient or highly proficient will go down, because they are deepening their understanding of what counts as high-quality teaching.	No expected impact in this first year. By next year, climate surveys will show that students are significantly more likely to report that their teachers care about and challenge them.

Consult with Others

Feedback from colleagues may be especially helpful when it comes to your plans to assess progress, especially regarding: (1) the likelihood that your data will help you track your progress in the ways you expect, and (2) ideas for how to marshal the assistance of others in data collection. The following protocol may be useful for this purpose:

1. Start with one plan to track progress and give your partner time to read your work.
2. Pose questions to solicit feedback, such as:
   - In your own words, what do you understand this plan involves in terms of measures and data collection?
   - How well have I specified actual measures of progress? How likely are those measures to help me understand my progress? Suggestions for improvement?
   - How likely are my data collection methods to help me assess my progress well? Am I drawing on existing data sources but also creating new ones?
   - Who else might be able to help me collect data?
   - Anything else?
3. Switch roles with your partner, providing them with feedback.
4. Repeat for your other progress tracking plan(s).
5. Use the feedback to improve your learning plan.

Reflect, Adjust, and Mark Your Calendar

Move the data collection tasks from your tracking plans into your work calendar and those of others who will help you with data collection. For example, remember that meeting you intended to conduct to practice engaging others in challenging conversations about racial equity? If someone will take notes for you at that meeting, make sure the meeting is on their calendar. Also put a reminder on your calendar to collect and clean up the notes, as necessary. At this time, you may want to set up a system for cataloging data over time.

4: TAKE ACTION

Taking action on your professional growth means ensuring you implement your learning and progress tracking plans and that you use your experience to make adjustments along the way. The following questions may help you think through how you will hold yourself accountable for following through on all three:

1. Will checking in with a partner help me hold myself accountable? If so, who should that partner be? When will we meet? What will I prepare for those meetings?
2. Will specifying a set day each month help me check in with a colleague and/or block out time for my own work and reflection? If so, which date? (Consider blocking out time on your calendar now.)
3. Since the adults I support should also be holding themselves accountable for taking their own actions, how might I model for them how I check in with myself about my learning plan and plan to assess progress and, in the process, make sure I am doing what I said I would do?
4. How will I use my meetings with my own supervisor to check in on the actions I am taking and my progress?

5: REASSESS AND BEGIN AGAIN

Even though you will have been monitoring your progress throughout the year, take time before you turn your mind to the next school year and return to part 1 and reassess your ability to lead along each of your standards. Now, you should have the benefit of more data to reflect on and, likely, to celebrate. If you are engaging in professional growth planning with your team, consider scheduling an end-of-year celebration to share areas for growth and lessons learned.

As you reassess, keep in mind the following:

- Don't wait. Complete an annual analysis of your work before this year ends when your data and experiences are fresher in your mind than they would be closer to the start of the next school year.

- Even though this is not your first time conducting your self-assessment, part 1 may take you longer each year if you have progressively more and better data.
- Your ratings may be lower now than they were at the start of the year. That's okay and potentially a good sign that you now understand your standards better and have a sharper sense of your own practice in relation to the standards.
- This professional growth planning process is yours to develop. How do you want to adapt this process to use next year? Consider making those shifts to your working protocols now while your experience is fresh in your mind.

EXHIBIT 4

Questions for Reflection and Discussion

Here we provide sample questions principal supervisors could use to reflect on their own practice and collaborate with colleagues to lead their learning together. Supervisors of principal supervisors and outside coaches might also use these questions and the relevant chapters as core texts in their efforts to support principal supervisors.

CHAPTER 1

Looking at the vignette:

1) In your own words, what is the principal supervisor doing in this case?
   a) How close is that way of working to how your district's principal supervisor(s) currently work? Main similarities? Differences?
   b) What difference, if any, do you think it makes for a principal when a principal supervisor works in the ways depicted in the vignette? Main upsides? Downsides?
   c) How does this vignette resonate with you?
   d) If you are a principal supervisor, what is one aspect of how the principal supervisor worked with her principal that especially excites or interests you? Why that one? Especially concerns you? Why that one?
      - If you work in a central office role other than principal supervisor, what would it mean for your role if your district's principal supervisor(s) worked like the principal supervisor featured in the vignette? What about your role could stay the same? What would need to change?
      - If you are a school principal, what would it look like and feel like if you had the principal supervisor in this vignette as your principal supervisor? What do you see the principal doing to support the shared goals of strengthening

principals' instructional leadership in the district? What especially resonates with you about that leadership role for school principals? Concerns you?

2) This chapter describes typical challenges school district central offices face in powerfully supporting excellent teaching and learning, especially for students school systems have historically underserved and marginalized.
   a) What are two or three of those challenges identified in this chapter?
   b) To what extent does your own district face those challenges? Main similarities? Differences?
3) Given those challenges, why central office transformation? What reasons do the authors give in this chapter? What do you think?
4) The authors say the shifts in principal supervision they studied were a part of a broader central office transformation initiative.
   a) How do the authors define central office transformation?
   b) In your own words, what is central office transformation?
   c) According to the authors, why is central office transformation important to the shifts in principal supervision? Do you agree? Disagree? Why or why not?
   d) According to the authors, why are the shifts in principal supervision an important part of central office transformation? Do you agree? Disagree? Why or why not?
5) The authors say that the shifts in principal supervision—to emphasize a teaching and learning approach to helping principals grow as instructional leaders—represent a transformation in that role.
   a) What do the authors mean by that?
   b) Do you agree or disagree? Why or why not?
   c) Thinking about the form of principal supervision the authors refer to as relatively new, how close is that way of working to how principal supervisors in your district work with principals? What are one or two examples that are similar? Different?

   d) What difference do you think it would make if your district's principal supervisors worked more like those in the positive cases in this volume? Main upsides? Any downsides?

6) What are two or three learning goals you have for yourself—and for your reading group, if you have one—as you work through this volume? Why those? How will you support each other in realizing those goals?

CHAPTERS 2 AND 3

Consider taking up this set of questions twice, once with a focus on principal supervisors' one-on-one work and a second time while reflecting on principals' meetings.

1) See question 1 under chapter 1 for questions relevant to exploring the vignette at the start of this chapter.
2) Looking at the section on helping principals lead their own learning through authentic tasks in real time:
   a) In your own words, what does helping principals lead their own learning in those ways entail?
   b) Why is helping principals lead their own learning essential to their actual growth as instructional leaders?
   c) What specific strategies are consistent with principal supervisors doing so?
   d) Which are inconsistent and ones to avoid?
   e) What are two or three concrete examples, if any, of how principal supervisors are already helping principals lead their own learning? What specifically are they doing in each example? How does each example reflect the definition of helping others strengthen their agency over their own learning?
   f) What are two or three concrete examples, if any, of how principal supervisors do not help principals lead their own learning or maybe get in the way of their doing so?
   g) What would take for your principal supervisors to make helping principals lead their own learning the core of what principal supervisors do? What support would principal supervisors need? What else would need to change?

3) Looking at the teaching and learning moves when principal supervisors directly support principal learning themselves, and working through each one:
   a) In your own words, what does this move entail?
   b) Why is such a move by mentors important for their learners' growth?
   c) Which one example from the subsection of that particular move most resonates with you? Why that one?
   d) Which one example from that subsection does not resonate or seems confusing or wrong?
   e) What would it take for your principal supervisors to make this move a more routine part of how they work directly with principals on their growth as instructional leaders? What support would principal supervisors need? What else would need to change?

CHAPTER 4

1) Looking at each of the specific conditions the researchers explored in relation to the positive and negative cases—prior knowledge, outside coaching, SPS mentoring, and principal supervisors leading their own learning—consider:
   a) In your own words, what does each condition involve?
   b) To what extent did each condition matter to the positive or negative cases? Why or why not?
   c) To what degree would you say principal supervisors in your district have access to the right supports for their success? Concrete examples for your assessment?
   d) What would it take to grow and deepen those supports for principal supervision in your district?
   e) What are specific steps you can take to enable and deepen those supports?
2) Repeat for each of the foundational conditions.

CHAPTER 5

1) Taking each one of the leaders (district leaders, principals, others) identified in this chapter as having an important role to play in advancing principal supervision as teaching and learning, consider:
   a) What specific next steps do the authors recommend these leaders take?
   b) Why those?
   c) Anything missing or that you otherwise would clarify or add?
   d) Looking across all those next steps—both those identified by the authors and generated by you—which two or three seem most important to advancing principal supervision as teaching and learning in your district? Why those?
   e) Which two or three seem next in importance? Why those?
   f) What concrete next steps will you or others take to ensure that those leaders take action on your priority recommendations?
   g) How will you continuously revisit and monitor your progress with advancing your priority recommendations?

Note on Methodology

The data from this volume come from two rigorous empirical investigations we conducted in nine school districts ranging in size from a subdistrict within New York City Public Schools with approximately two hundred thousand students to rural districts with two to five thousand students (see table 1.1). As we discussed in chapter 1, we selected these districts because leaders in each seemed to understand the fundamental mismatch between their long-standing central office practices and systems and what districtwide teaching and learning improvement would take. They all aimed to redesign their entire central office toward those results, with shifts in the principal supervisor role as an integral part. And they all worked with outside support organizations to provide professional development opportunities for principal supervisors and otherwise support the transformation process. All but three of the forty principal supervisors in these districts chose to participate in our studies, suggesting minimal selection bias within districts.[1]

DATA SOURCES

Given the complexity of central office transformation and the limitations of interviews and other self-report data for understanding shifts in professional practice, we relied on real-time observations as our main data source in both studies. Over the course of thirty-six months we spent 763.75 hours directly observing leaders as they engaged in central office transformation. About 60 percent of those hours included such settings as principal supervisors' formal and informal meetings with each other, meetings principal supervisors ran for their principals that were supposed to function as professional learning communities, and other meetings related to the central office transformation process in each district (e.g., cabinet sessions) in which principal supervisors participated or generally were a topic of conversation. In several districts we also shadowed principal supervisors as they worked with their principals and, sometimes, outside coaches.

Given the nascent state of scholarship on principal supervision and leadership as teaching and learning more broadly, during meeting observations, we took verbatim notes to help ensure we captured as much of principal supervisors' actual work as possible. Where relevant, we also created low-inference descriptions of other aspects of meetings such as late arrivals, facial expressions, and tone of voice. For the shadowing, we typically used an audiorecorder to capture conversations and side conversations with principal supervisors as they unfolded in real time. We then transcribed those recordings for later coding.

We supplemented those observations with 340 semistructured interviews with principal supervisors, other central office administrators, school principals, and outside coaches over time. We probed for people's understanding of the new principal supervisors' role and what they had seen of that role in practice. To sample principals, we asked each principal supervisor which principals they worked with most and least frequently. We then interviewed those principals to capture a range of interactions with, and principal views about, their supervisors.

We also collected and reviewed hundreds of documents from each district that revealed how principal supervisors went about their work. For example, we reviewed principal supervisors' calendars, their email communications with principals, and readings, tools, and other materials they used when working with principals.

DATA ANALYSIS

We used NVivo data analysis software to analyze our data from each study through several stages. First, we sorted our data into low-inference categories such as "principal outcomes," "principal supervisor A," and "conditions of principal supervisors' work." During this phase, we took the general definitions of degrees of appropriation and translated them into observable markers specific to principal supervisors taking a progressively deeper teaching and learning approach to their work.

In phase 2, we went into our sorted data with our outcomes scale and other higher inference codes derived from our conceptual framework. For instance, we resorted the "principal outcomes" data with categories consistent with degrees of appropriation, such as principals' progressively deeper engagement in more complex instructional leadership tasks. For the principal supervisor data, we used categories from our conceptual framework such as "modeling," "talk," and "other"—the latter to ensure we were remaining open to principal supervisors' engagement in tasks other than those in our conceptual framework. In each category, we distinguished examples as reflecting the varying degrees of appropriation. Through a process of constant comparison, we identified four types of principal supervisors' practice. We then looked at the data on principal outcomes alongside the data on the practice of their principal supervisor and found the clear relationships we describe in this volume.

In phase 3, we went back to the data we had coded as "conditions" related to how principal supervisors worked and used higher-inference concepts from our conceptual framework to further sort the data. We arrayed the conditions by type of principal supervisor practice to see if we could find any consistencies between the pattern of types and the conditions.

Our methods do not allow us to claim causation—that certain forms of principal supervision produced particular outcomes for principals, or that particular conditions caused principal supervisors to operate in certain ways. However, the consistency of the patterns with socio-cultural theories lend strong support for the associations we identify in this book. We use the term "association" to refer to the relationship between principal supervisors' practice and conditions to distinguish that relationship from causation.

Throughout, we held ourselves to the high standard of substantiating all findings with at least three different data sources. In addition, as we have mentioned, we not only researched principal supervision, but also worked alongside principal supervisors ourselves in district and district networks that have invited us to help them learn about this line of research and use it in their practice. Where consistent with our main findings, we brought in examples from those districts if we thought those examples clearly and concisely illustrated our primary claims.

REPORTING IN THIS VOLUME

All quotes in the main text of this volume are verbatim directly from our dataset. The vignettes at the start of each chapter also stem directly from our data, but we developed them as composite pictures—drawing on data across principal supervisor cases—to present a single, anchoring example for each chapter. We developed the quotes in the vignettes by combining and streamlining principal supervisors' actual statements.

Notes

Chapter 1

1. All formal names are pseudonyms. Throughout the volume, we randomly assigned principal supervisors he/she pronouns to further protect the confidentiality of our respondents. The vignettes that start each chapter are composite examples of principal supervisors working at high levels in particular ways. For more on how we constructed these vignettes, please see the methodological appendix.
2. Gregory F. Branch, Eric A. Hanushek, and Steven G. Rivkin, *Estimating the Effect of Leaders on Public Sector Productivity: The Case of School Principals* (Washington, DC: National Center for Analysis of Longitudinal Data in Education Research, 2012); Kenneth Leithwood et al., *Review of Research: How Leadership Influences Student Learning* (Minneapolis: University of Minnesota, Center for Applied Research and Educational Improvement, 2004); Christine Neumerski, "Rethinking Instructional Leadership, A Review: What Do We Know About Principal, Teacher, and Coach Instructional Leadership, and Where Should We Go from Here?" *Educational Administration Quarterly* 49, no. 2 (2012).
3. Andrew Croft et al., *Job-Embedded Professional Development: What It Is, Who Is Responsible, and How to Get It Done Well. Issue Brief* (Washington DC: National Comprehensive Center for Teacher Quality, 2010); Elaine Fink and Lauren B. Resnick, "Developing Principals as Instructional Leaders," *Phi Delta Kappan* 82, no. 8 (2001): 598–610; Pamela Grossman et al., "Teaching Practice: A Cross-Professional Perspective," *Teachers College Record* 111, no. 9 (2009): 2055–100; Meredith I. Honig, "District Central Office Leadership as Teaching: How Central Office Administrators Support Principals' Development as Instructional Leaders," *Educational Administration Quarterly*, 48, no. 4 (2012): 733–74; Meredith I. Honig and Lydia R. Rainey, "Central Office Leadership in Principal Professional Learning Communities: The Practice Beneath the Policy," *Teachers College Record* 116,

no. 4 (2014): 733–74; Sally J. Zepeda, Oksana Parylo, and Ed Bengtson, "Analyzing Principal Professional Development Practices Through the Lens of Adult Learning Theory," *Professional Development in Education* 40, no. 2 (2014): 295–315.

4. Amanda Corcoran et al., *Rethinking Leadership: The Changing Role of Principal Supervisors* (Washington, DC: Council of the Great City Schools, 2013); Ellen B. Goldring et al., *A New Role Emerges for Principal Supervisors: Evidence from Six Districts in the Principal Supervisor Initiative* (Nashville: Peabody College, Vanderbilt University, 2018); Meredith I. Honig et al., *Central Office Transformation for District-wide Teaching and Learning Improvement* (Seattle: Center for Teaching and Policy, College of Education, University of Washington, 2010); Rebecca A. Thessin, "Establishing Productive Principal/Principal Supervisor Partnerships for Instructional Leadership," *Journal of Educational Administration* 57, no. 5 (2019); Brenda J. Turnbull, Derek L. Riley, and Jaclyn R. MacFarlane, *Districts Taking Charge of the Principal Pipeline* (Washington, DC: Policy Study Associates, 2015).
5. Corcoran et al., *Rethinking Leadership*; Goldring et al., *A New Role Emerges*; Thessin, "Establishing Productive Principal/Principal Supervisor Partnerships; Turnbull et al., *Districts Taking Charge*.
6. Ellen Goldring et al., "Make Room Value Added: Principals' Human Capital Decisions and the Emergence of Teacher Observation Data," *Educational Researcher* 44, no. 2 (2015): 96–104; Jason A. Grissom and Susanna Loeb, "Triangulating Principal Effectiveness: How Perspectives of Parents, Teachers, and Assistant Principals Identify the Central Importance of Managerial Skills," *American Educational Research Journal* 48, no. 5 (2011): 1091–123; Jason A. Grissom, "Can Good Principals Keep Teachers in Disadvantaged Schools? Linking Principal Effectiveness to Teacher Satisfaction and Turnover in Hard-to-Staff Environments," *Teachers College Record* 113, no. 11 (2011): 2552–85; Jason A. Grissom and Brendan Bartanen, "Strategic Retention: Principal Effectiveness and Teacher Turnover in Multiple-Measure Teacher Evaluation Systems," *American Educational Research Journal* 56, no. 2 (2019): 514–55; Eileen Horng and Susanna Loeb, "New Thinking About Instructional Leadership," *Phi Delta Kappan* 92, no. 3 (2010): 66–69.
7. Leithwood et al., *Review of Research*, 3.
8. Branch et al., *Estimating the Effect*; Philip Hallinger and Joseph Murphy, "Assessing the Instructional Management Behavior of Principals," *Elementary School Journal* 86, no. 2 (1985): 217–47; Philip Hallinger et al., "Identifying the Specific Practices, Behaviors for Principals," *NASSP Bulletin* 67, no. 463 (1983): 83–91; Ronald H. Heck, "Principals' Instructional Leadership and School Performance: Implications for Policy Development," *Educational Evaluation and Policy Analysis* 14, no. 1 (1992): 21–34; Leithwood et al., *Review of Research*; Helen M. Marks and Susan M. Printy, "Principal

Leadership and School Performance: An Integration of Transformational and Instructional Leadership," *Educational Administration Quarterly* 39, no. 3 (2003): 370–97; Neumerski, "Rethinking."

9. Judith Kafka, "The Principalship in Historical Perspective," *Peabody Journal of Education* 84, no. 3 (2009): 318–30; Deborah L. West, Craig Peck, and Ulrich C. Reitzug, "Limited Control and Relentless Accountability: Examining Historical Changes in Urban School Principal Pressure," *Journal of School Leadership* 20, no. 2 (2010).
10. Lawrence A. Cremin, *American Education: The National Experience* (New York: Harper & Row, 1980); Lawrence A. Cremin, *Popular Education and Its Discontents* (New York: Harper & Row, 1990); Larry Cuban, *The Managerial Imperative and the Practice of Leadership in Schools* (Albany: State University of New York Press, 1988); David A. Gamson and Emily M. Hodge, "Education Research and the Shifting Landscape of the American School District, 1816 to 2016," *Review of Research in Education* 40, no. 1 (2016): 216–49; Jeffrey Mirel, *The Rise and Fall of the Urban School System: Detroit, 1907–81*, 2nd ed. (Ann Arbor: University of Michigan Press, 1999); Tracy L. Steffes, "Solving the 'Rural School Problem': New State Aid, Standards, and Supervision of Local Schools, 1900–1933," *History of Education Quarterly* 48, no. 2 (2008): 181–220; David B. Tyack, *The One Best System: A History of American Urban Education* (Cambridge, MA: Harvard University Press, 1974); David B. Tyack and Larry Cuban, *Tinkering Toward Utopia* (Cambridge, MA: Harvard University Press, 1995).
11. Cuban, *The Managerial Imperative.*
12. Edwin Bridges, "Research on the School Administrator: The State of the Art, 1967–1980," *Educational Administration Quarterly* 18, no. 3 (1982): 12–33; Philip Hallinger and Joseph Murphy, "Assessing the Instructional Management Behavior of Principals," *Elementary School Journal* 86, no. 2 (1985): 217–47; Philip Hallinger et al., "Effective Schools: The Specific Policies and Practices of the Principal," *National Association of Secondary School Principals Bulletin* 67, no. 1 (1983): 83–91; Viviane M. Robinson, Claire A. Lloyd, and Kenneth J. Rowe, "The Impact of Leadership on Student Outcomes: An Analysis of the Differential Effects of Leadership Types," *Educational Administration Quarterly* 44, no. 5 (2008).
13. CCSSO refreshed their national standards for school leadership in 2008 and then again in 2015 to further underscore principals' instructional focus and specifically name the importance of their leading for educational equity. "Standards for School Leaders," Council of Chief State School Officers, 1996; "Educational Leadership Policy Standards: ISLLC 2008," Council of Chief State School Officers, 2008, https://www.danforth.uw.edu/uw danforth/media/danforth/isllc-2008.pdf.
14. "ESEA Title II," US Department of Education, https://www2.ed.gov/policy /elsec/leg/essa/legislation/title-ii.pdf; "Race to the Top Summary," US

Department of Education, https://www2.ed.gov/programs/racetothetop/executive-summary.pdf.

15. James Sebastian and Elaine Allensworth, "The Influence of Principal Leadership on Classroom Instruction and Student Learning: A Study of Mediated Pathways to Learning," *Educational Administration Quarterly* 48, no. 4 (2012): 626–63, 643.
16. Jason A. Grissom, Susanna Loeb, and Benjamin Master, "Effective Instructional Time Use for School Leaders: Longitudinal Evidence from Observations of Principals," *Educational Researcher* 42, no. 8 (2013): 433–44; Karen Seashore Louis et al., *Investigating the Links to Improved Student Learning: Final Report of Research Findings* (Minneapolis: University of Minnesota, Center for Applied Research and Educational Improvement, 2010). See also Cheryl Graczewski, Joel Knudson, and Deborah J. Holtzman, "Instructional Leadership in Practice: What Does It Look Like, and What Influence Does It Have?" *Journal of Education for Students Placed At Risk* 14, no. 1 (2009): 72–96; Joseph Blase and Jo Blase, "Principals' Instructional Leadership and Teacher Development: Teachers' Perspectives," *Educational Administration Quarterly* 35, no. 3 (1999): 349–78; Christine Neumerski et al., "Restructuring Instructional Leadership: How Multiple-Measure Teacher Evaluation Systems Are Redefining the Role of the School Principal," *Elementary School Journal* 119, no. 2 (2018): 270–97; Jessica Rigby, "Principals' Sensemaking and Enactment of Teacher Evaluation," *Journal of Educational Administration* 53 no. 3 (2015), 374–92.
17. Hans Klar et al., "Fostering the Capacity for Distributed Leadership: A Post-Heroic Approach to Leading School Improvement," *International Journal of Leadership in Education* 19, no. 2 (2016): 111–37; Hans W. Klar, "Fostering Department Chair Instructional Leadership Capacity: Laying the Groundwork for Distributed Instructional Leadership," *International Journal of Leadership in Education* 15, no. 2 (2012); Hans W. Klar, "Fostering Distributed Instructional Leadership: A Sociocultural Perspective of Leadership Development in Urban High Schools," *Leadership and Policy in Schools* 11, no. 4 (2012); Melinda M. Mangin, "Facilitating Elementary Principals' Support for Instructional Teacher Leadership," *Educational Administration Quarterly* 43, no. 3 (2007): 319–57; Neumerski, "Rethinking"; Susan M. Printy, "Leadership for Teacher Learning: A Community of Practice Perspective," *Educational Administration Quarterly* 44, no. 2 (2008): 187–226; Aimee LaPointe Terosky, "From a Managerial Imperative to a Learning Imperative: Experiences of Urban, Public School Principals," *Educational Administration Quarterly* 50, no. 1 (2014): 3–33; Jonathan Supovitz, Philip Sirinides, and Henry May, "How Principals and Peers Influence Teaching and Learning," *Educational Administration Quarterly* 46, no. 1 (2010): 31–56.

18. Blase and Blase, "Principals Instructional Leadership"; Printy, "Leadership"; Elizabeth Leisy Stosich, Candice Bocala, and Michelle Forman, "Building Coherence for Instructional Improvement Through Professional Development: A Design-Based Implementation Research Study," *Educational Management Administration & Leadership* 46, no. 5 (2018): 864–80.
19. Rekha Balu, Eileen L. Horng, and Susanna Loeb, "Strategic Personnel Management: How School Principals Recruit, Retain, Develop and Remove Teachers," *School Leadership Research*, working paper (2010): 10–16; Julia Koppich and Connie Showalter, *Strategic Management of Human Capital: Crosscase Analysis* (Philadelphia: University of Pennsylvania, Consortium for Policy Research in Education, 2008); Goldring et al., "Make Room"; Grissom and Loeb, "Triangulating"; Grissom, "Good Principals"; Grissom and Bartanen, "Strategic Retention."
20. Grissom and Bartanen, "Strategic Retention."
21. Muhammad A. Khalifa, Mark Anthony Gooden, and James Earl Davis, "Culturally Responsive School Leadership: A Synthesis of the Literature," *Review of Educational Research* 86, no. 4 (2016): 1272–311.
22. Bradley W. Carpenter and Sarah Diem, "Guidance Matters: A Critical Discourse Analysis of the Race-Related Policy Vocabularies Shaping Leadership Preparation," *Urban Education* 50, no. 5 (2015): 515–34; Bradley W. Davis, Mark A. Gooden, and Donna J. Micheaux, "Color-Blind Leadership: A Critical Race Theory Analysis of the ISLLC and ELCC Standards," *Educational Administration Quarterly* 51, no. 3 (2015): 335–71; Mollie K. Galloway and Ann M. Ishimaru, "Radical Recentering: Equity in Educational Leadership Standards," *Educational Administration Quarterly* 51, no. 3 (2015): 372–408; Mollie K. Galloway and Ann M. Ishimaru, "Equitable Leadership on the Ground: Converging on High-Leverage Practices," *Education Evaluation and Policy Analysis* 25, no. 2 (2017): 1–33; Mark A. Gooden and Michael Dantley, "Centering Race in a Framework for Leadership Preparation," *Journal of Research on Leadership Education* 7, no. 2 (2012): 237–53; Khalifa et al., "Culturally Responsive School Leadership."
23. Galloway and Ishimaru, "Radical Recentering"; Galloway and Ishimaru, "Equitable Leadership"; Luis C. Moll et al., "Funds of Knowledge for Teaching: Using a Qualitative Approach to Connect Homes and Classrooms," *Theory into Practice* 31, no. 2 (1992): 132–41; Khalifa et al., "Culturally Responsive School Leadership"; Martin Scanlan and Francesca López, "¡Vamos! How School Leaders Promote Equity and Excellence for Bilingual Students," *Educational Administration Quarterly* 48, no. 4 (2012): 583–625; George Theoharis, "Social Justice Educational Leaders and Resistance: Toward a Theory of Social Justice Leadership," *Educational Administration Quarterly* 43, no. 2 (2007): 221–58.
24. The Wallace Foundation, *The School Principal as Leader: Guiding Schools to Better Teaching and Learning* (New York: The Wallace Foundation, 2012).

25. Aimee LaPointe Terosky, "From a Managerial Imperative to a Learning Imperative: Experiences of Urban, Public School Principals," *Educational Administration Quarterly* 50, no. 1 (2014).
26. Richard F. Elmore and Deanna Burney, *Investing in Teacher Learning: Staff Development and Instructional Improvement in Community School District #2, New York City* (New York: National Commission on Teaching & America's Future, 1997); Fink and Resnick, "Developing Principals."
27. See, for example, Meredith I. Honig, "No Small Thing: School District Central Office Bureaucracies and the Implementation of New Small Autonomous Schools Initiatives," *American Education Research Journal* 46, no. 2 (2009): 387–422; Meredith I. Honig and Lydia R. Rainey, "Autonomy and School Improvement: What Do We Know and Where Do We Go From Here?" *Educational Policy* 26, no. 3 (2015): 465–95; Lea Hubbard, Hugh Mehan, and Mary Kay Stein, *Reform as Learning: When School Reform Collided with Organizational Culture and Community Politics in San Diego* (New York: Routledge, 2006); Betty Malen, Rodney T. Ogawa, and Jennifer Kranz, "What Do We Know About School-Based Management? A Case Study of the Literature—A Call for Research," *Choice and Control in American Education* 2 (1990): 289–342; Stewart C. Purkey and Marshall S. Smith, "School Reform: The District Policy Implications of the Effective Schools Literature," *Elementary School Journal* 85, no. 3 (1985): 353–89.
28. Mark Berends, Susan J. Bodilly, and Sheila Nataraj Kirby, "The Future of Whole School Designs: Conclusions, Observations, and Policy Implications," in *Facing the Challenges of Whole School Reform: New American Schools After a Decade*, ed. Mark Berends et al. (Santa Monica: RAND Education, 2002), 142–54.
29. Malen et al., "School-Based Management."
30. James P. Spillane, "State Policy and the Non-Monolithic Nature of the Local School District: Organizational and Professional Considerations," *American Educational Research Journal* 35 no. 1 (1998): 33–63; James P. Spillane, "Cognition and Policy Implementation: District Policymakers and the Reform of Mathematics Education," *Cognition and Instruction* 18, no. 2 (2000): 141–79; James P. Spillane and Karen A. Callahan, "Implementing State Standards for Science Education: What District Policy Makers Make of the Hoopla," *Journal of Research in Science Teaching* 37, no. 5 (2000): 401–25; James P. Spillane and Charles L. Thompson, "Reconstructing Conceptions of Local Capacity: The Local Education Agency's Capacity for Ambitious Instructional Reform," *Educational Evaluation and Policy Analysis* 19, no. 2 (1997): 185–203; James P. Spillane and John S. Zeuli, "Reform and Teaching: Exploring Patterns of Practice in the Context of National and State Mathematics Reforms," *Educational Evaluation and Policy Analysis* 21, no. 1 (1999); Hubbard et al., *Reform as Learning*.
31. Tina Trujillo, "The Politics of District Instructional Policy Formation: Compromising Equity and Rigor," *Educational Policy* 27, no. 3 (2013): 531–59;

Tina Trujillo and Sarah L. Woulfin, "Equity-Oriented Reform Amid Standards-Based Accountability: A Qualitative Comparative Analysis of an Intermediary's Instructional Practices," *American Educational Research Journal* 51, no. 2 (2014): 253–93.

32. Alan J. Daly and Kara S. Finnigan, "The Ebb and Flow of Social Network Ties Between District Leaders Under High-Stakes Accountability," *American Educational Research Journal* 48, no. 1 (2011): 39–79; Alan J. Daly and Kara S. Finnigan , "Exploring the Space Between: Social Networks, Trust, and Urban School District Leaders," *Journal of School Leadership* 22, no. 3 (2012): 493–530; Jackie Mania-Singer, "A Systems Theory Approach to the District Central Office's Role in School-Level Improvement," *Administrative Issues Journal: Connecting Education, Practice, and Research* 7, no. 1 (2017): 70–83.
33. Cremin, *Popular Education*; Mirel, *The Rise and Fall*; Steffes, "Solving"; Tyack, *One Best System*; Tyack and Cuban, *Tinkering*; Gamson and Hodge, "Shifting Landscape."
34. Edward John Fuller and Michelle D. Young, *Tenure and Retention of Newly Hired Principals in Texas* (Austin: University Council for Educational Administration, Department of Educational Administration, University of Texas at Austin, 2009); Grissom, "Good Principals"; Susanna Loeb, Demetra Kalogrides, and Eileen Lai Horng, "Principal Preferences and the Uneven Distribution of Principals Across Schools," *Educational Evaluation and Policy Analysis* 32, no. 2 (2010): 205–29; Stephanie Levin and Kathryn Bradley, *Understanding and Addressing Principal Turnover: A Review of the Research* (Palo Alto, CA: Learning Policy Institute, 2019); Rui Yan, "The Influence of Working Conditions on Principal Turnover in K–12 Public Schools," *Educational Administration Quarterly* (2019).
35. Meredith I. Honig et al., *Central Office Transformation for District-wide Teaching and Learning Improvement* (Seattle: Center for the Study of Teaching and Policy, 2010); Honig, "Leadership as Teaching"; Honig and Rainey, "Principal Professional Learning Communities."
36. Blase and Blase, "Principals Instructional Leadership"; Tricia Browne-Ferrigno and Rodney Muth, "Leadership Mentoring and Situated Learning," *Mentoring & Tutoring: Partnership in Learning* 14 no. 3 (2006), Croft et al., *Job-Embedded Professional Development*; Fink and Resnick, "Developing Principals"; Leithwood et al., *Review of Research*; Kent Peterson, "The Professional Development of Principals: Innovations and Opportunities," *Educational Administration Quarterly* 38, no. 2 (2002), 213–32; Zepeda et al., "Principal Professional Development"; Kent Peterson, "The Professional Development of Principals: Innovations and Opportunities," *Educational Administration Quarterly* 38, no. 2 (2002): 213–32; Carol A. Barnes et al., "Developing Instructional Leaders: Using Mixed Methods to Explore the Black Box of Planned Change in Principals' Professional Practice," *Educational Administration Quarterly* 46, no. 2

(2010): 241–79; Eleanor Drago-Severson, "Teaching, Learning and Leading in Today's Complex World: Reaching New Heights with a Developmental Approach," *International Journal of Leadership in Education* 19, no. 1 (2016): 56–86; Bradley Portin et al., *Leadership for Learning Improvement in Urban Schools* (Seattle: Center for the Study of Teaching and Policy, University of Washington, 2009); Elizabeth A. City et al., *Instructional Rounds in Education: A Network Approach to Improving Teaching and Learning* (Cambridge: Harvard Education Press, 2009); John Seely Brown, Allan Collins, and Paul Duguid, "Situated Cognition and the Culture of Learning," *Educational Researcher* 18, no. 1 (1989): 32–42; Jean Lave, "Situating Learning in Communities of Practice," in *Perspectives on Socially Shared Cognition*, ed. Lauren Resnick et al. (Washington, DC: American Psychological Association, 1991).

37. Elmore and Burney, Investing in Teacher Learning; Richard F. Elmore and Deanna Burney, School Variation and Systemic Instructional Improvement in Community School District #2, New York City (New York: Learning Research and Development Center, 1997); Richard F. Elmore and Deanna Burney, Continuous Improvement in Community District #2, New York City (Philadelphia: University of Pennsylvania, CPRE, 1998); Richard F. Elmore and Deanna Burney, Leadership and Learning: Principal Recruitment, Induction and Instructional Leadership in Community School District #2, New York City (Philadelphia: University of Pennsylvania, CPRE, 2000); Fink and Resnick, "Developing Principals"; Amy M. Hightower, School Districts and Instructional Renewal (New York: Teachers College Press, 2002).
38. Elmore and Burney, *Leadership and Learning*; Fink and Resnick, "Developing Principals."
39. Catherine H. Augustine et al., *Improving School Leadership: The Promise of Cohesive Leadership Systems* (Santa Monica, CA: RAND Education, 2009). See also Min Sun and Peter Youngs. "How Does District Principal Evaluation Affect Learning-Centered Principal Leadership? Evidence from Michigan School Districts," *Leadership and Policy in Schools* 8, no. 4 (2009): 411–45.
40. Stephen Andersson et al., "No One Way: Differentiating School District Leadership and Support for School Improvement," *Journal of Educational Change* 13, no. 4 (2012).
41. See, for example, Roland G. Tharp and Ronald Gallimore *Rousing Minds to Life: Teaching, Learning, and Schooling in Social Context* (Cambridge, UK: Cambridge University Press, 1991); Etienne Wenger, *Communities of Practice: Learning, Meaning, and Identity* (Cambridge, UK: Cambridge University Press, 1999).
42. Tharp and Gallimore, *Rousing Minds.*
43. Barbara Rogoff et al., "First-Hand Learning Through Intent Participation," *Annual Review of Psychology* 54 (2003); Angela Calabrese Barton and

Edna Tan, "'We Be Burnin'!' Agency, Identity, and Science Learning," *Journal of the Learning Sciences* 19, no. 2 (2010).

44. Croft et al., Job-Embedded Professional Development.
45. Barbara Rogoff et al., "Development Through Participation in Sociocultural Activity," in *New Directions for Child Development, No. 67: Cultural Practices as Contexts for Development*, ed. Jacqueline J. Goodnow, Peggy J. Miller, and Frank Kessel (San Francisco: Jossey-Bass, 1995): 45–65; Jean Lave and Etienne Wenger, *Situated Learning: Legitimate Peripheral Participation* (Cambridge, UK: Cambridge University Press, 1991); Peter Smagorinsky, Leslie Susan Cook, and Tara Star Johnson, *The Twisting Path of Concept Development in Learning To Teach. Report Series* (Albany: State University of New York, 2003); Wenger, *Communities of Practice.*
46. Anthony Bryk and Barbara Schneider, *Trust in Schools: A Core Resource for Improvement* (New York: Russell Sage Foundation, 2002).
47. Ann L. Brown and Joseph C. Campione, "Guided Discovery in a Community of Learners," in *Classroom Lessons: Integrating Cognitive Theory and Classroom Practice*, ed. Kate McGilly (Cambridge, MA: MIT Press/Bradford, 1994), 229; Tharp and Gallimore, *Rousing Minds.*
48. Allan M. Collins, John Seely Brown, and Ann Holum, "Cognitive Apprenticeship: Making Thinking Visible," *American Educator* 15, no. 3 (1991): 2.
49. Brown et al., "Situated Cognition."
50. Collins et al., "Cognitive Apprenticeship."
51. Ilana Seidel Horn and Judith Warren Little, "Attending to Problems of Practice: Routines and Resources for Professional Learning in Teachers' Workplace Interactions," *American Educational Research Journal* 47, no. 1 (2010): 181–217.
52. Dorothy C. Holland et al., *Identity and Agency in Cultural Worlds* (Cambridge, MA: Harvard University Press, 2001); Lave and Wenger, *Situated Learning*; Wenger, *Communities of Practice.*
53. Wenger, Communities of Practice.
54. Wenger, Communities of Practice.
55. Lave and Wenger, Situated Learning; Wenger, Communities of Practice.
56. John D. Bransford, Ann L. Brown, and Rodney R. Cocking, *How People Learn: Brain, Mind, Experience, and School* (Washington, DC: National Academy Press, 2000); Carol S. Dweck, *Mindset: The New Psychology of Success* (New York, Random House, 2008).
57. Holland et al., *Identity and Agency.*
58. Tharp and Gallimore, *Rousing Minds.*
59. Lauren B. Resnick, "From Aptitude to Effort: A New Foundation for Our Schools," *American Educator* 23, no. 1 (1999): 14–17.
60. National Academies of Sciences, Engineering, and Medicine, *How People Learn II: Learners, Contexts, and Cultures* (Washington, DC: National Academies Press, 2018).

61. Grossman et al., "Teaching Practice."
62. Bransford et al., *How People Learn.*
63. David K. Cohen, "A Revolution in One Classroom: The Case of Mrs. Oublier," *Education Evaluation and Policy Analysis* 12, no. 3 (1990): 311–29.
64. Cynthia E. Coburn and Mary Kay Stein, *Research and Practice in Education: Building Alliances, Bridging the Divide* (Lanham: Rowman & Littlefield Publishers, 2010); Meredith I. Honig, "The New Middle Management: Intermediary Organizations in Education Policy Implementation," *Educational Evaluation and Policy Analysis* 26 no. 1 (2004): 65–87.

Chapter 2

1. Per the Note on Methodology, we sampled principals by asking each principal supervisor to discuss two principals with whom they worked intensively and two less so. This strategy yielded a sample that primarily consisted of principals who at the start displayed limited instructional leadership (typically the ones with whom principal supervisors worked most often) and those who displayed higher levels (generally those with whom supervisors worked relatively less often).

Chapter 4

1. When we asked about the principal supervisors in the "traditional" cases—who actually had prior experience largely outside education in business consulting and other arenas—the leader explained that they were part of an initial experiment in the district to explore the kinds of professionals who could be successful with the new principal supervisor role.
2. In smaller systems, the superintendent/principal supervisor reports directly to the school board. Because such hands-on coaching is beyond the scope of a school board's role, we did not include the smaller districts in this part of our analysis. For more on this distinction about the role of school boards, see T. L. Alsbury and P. Gore, eds., *Improving School Board Effectiveness: A Balanced Governance Approach* (Cambridge, MA: Harvard Education Press, 2015).

Chapter 5

1. Enrique Alemán Jr., "Is Robin Hood the 'Prince of Thieves' or a Pathway to Equity? Applying Critical Race Theory to School Finance Political Discourse," *Educational Policy* 20, no. 1 (2006): 113–42; Tina M. Trujillo, "The Politics of District Instructional Policy Formation: Compromising Equity and Rigor," *Educational Policy* 27, no. 3 (2013): 531–59; Sue Feldman and Ilana Winchester, "Racial-Equity Policy as Leadership Practice: Using Social Practice Theory to Analyze Policy as Practice," *International Journal of Multicultural Education* 17, no. 1 (2015): 62–81; Ann Curry-Stevens, Analucia Lopezrevoredo, and Dana Peters, *Policies to Eliminate*

Racial Disparities in Education: A Literature Review (Portland, OR: Center to Advance Racial Equity, Portland State University, 2013); Mollie K. Galloway and Ann M. Ishimaru, "Radical Recentering: Equity in Educational Leadership Standards," *Educational Administration Quarterly* 51, no. 3 (2015): 372–408.

2. Lisa Delpit, "Other People's Children: Cultural Conflict in the Classroom," *Harvard Educational Review* 65 (1995): 510–10; Jonathan Kozol, *The Shame of the Nation: The Restoration of Apartheid Schooling in America* (New York: Broadway Books, 2005); Gloria Ladson-Billings, "From the Achievement Gap to the Education Debt: Understanding Achievement in US Schools," *Educational Researcher* 35, no. 7 (2006): 3–12.
3. John B. Diamond, "Race and White Supremacy in the Sociology of Education: Shifting the Intellectual Gaze," in *Education in a New Society: Renewing the Sociology of Education*, ed. Jal Mehta and Scott Davies (Chicago: University of Chicago Press, 2018), 345; Adrienne D. Dixson and Celia Rousseau Anderson, "Where Are We? Critical Race Theory in Education 20 Years Later," *Peabody Journal of Education* 93, no. 1 (2018): 121–31; Mollie K. Galloway and Ann M. Ishimaru, "Equitable Leadership on the Ground: Converging on High-Leverage Practices," *Education Policy Analysis Archives/Archivos Analíticos de Políticas Educativas* 25 (2017): 1–36; Mark A. Gooden and Michael Dantley, "Centering Race in a Framework for Leadership Preparation," *Journal of Research on Leadership Education* 7, no. 2 (2012): 237–53: Muhammad Khalifa, Christopher Dunbar, and Ty-Ron Douglas, "Derrick Bell, CRT, and Educational Leadership 1995–Present," *Race Ethnicity and Education* 16, no. 4 (2013): 489–513; Muhammad A. Khalifa, Mark Anthony Gooden, and James Earl Davis, "Culturally Responsive School Leadership: A Synthesis of the Literature," *Review of Educational Research* 86, no. 4 (2016): 1272–1311; Gloria Ladson-Billings, "Critical Race Theory—What It Is Not!" in *Handbook of Critical Race Theory in Education*, ed. Marvin Lynn and Adrienne D. Dixson (New York: Routledge, 2013), 54–67; Sherry Marx and Larry L. Larson, "Taking Off the Color-Blind Glasses: Recognizing and Supporting Latina/o Students in a Predominantly White School," *Educational Administration Quarterly* 48, no. 2 (2012): 259–303; Eve Tuck, "Suspending Damage: A Letter to Communities," *Harvard Educational Review* 79, no. 3 (2009): 409–28; James Wright et al., "The Color of Neoliberal Reform: A Critical Race Policy Analysis of School District Takeovers in Michigan," *Urban Education* (November 2018), https://doi.org/10.1177/0042085918806943.
4. Lisa Bass, "When Care Trumps Justice: The Operationalization of Black Feminist Caring in Educational Leadership," *International Journal of Qualitative Studies in Education* 25, no. 1 (2012): 73–87; Lorri J. Santamaría and Jean-Marie Gaëtane, "Cross-Cultural Dimensions of Applied, Critical, and

Transformational Leadership: Women Principals Advancing Social Justice and Educational Equity," *Cambridge Journal of Education* 44, no. 3 (2014): 333–60; David E. DeMatthews et al., "Guilty as Charged? Principals' Perspectives on Disciplinary Practices and the Racial Discipline Gap," *Educational Administration Quarterly* 53, no. 4 (2017): 519–55.

Appendix

1. For a downloadable copy of these standards, see http://dl2.education.uw.edu/resources/principal-supervisors/.
2. These items were adapted from the validated instruments in District Leadership Design Lab, *Annual Surveys of Principals and Principal Supervisors: A Guide for District Leaders* (Seattle: District Leadership Design Lab, College of Education, University of Washington, 2018).
3. For a full downloadable copy of this tool, see http://dl2.education.uw.edu/resources/principal-supervisors/.
4. For sample data sources for each standard, see http://dl2.education.uw.edu/wp-content/uploads/2017/07/2017-DL2-Principal-Supervisor-Performance-Standards-INDICATORS-2.0.pdf.
5. Council of Chief State School Officers, *Model Principal Supervisor Performance Standards 2015* (Washington, DC: CCSSO, 2015). These standards incorporate earlier versions of our principal supervisor performance standards and add two others.
6. We validated related survey items by asking specifically about how principal supervisors provide feedback to their principals. District leaders may want to add a version of these items that asks specifically about principal supervisors' provision of feedback and/or localize the high-inference terminology "talk moves" that we use in the presentation of findings in this volume.

Note on Methodology

1. For more on our site selection strategies, see Meredith I. Honig, "District Central Office Leadership as Teaching: How Central Office Administrators Support Principals' Development as Instructional Leaders," *Educational Administration Quarterly* 48, no. 4 (2012): 733–74; Meredith I. Honig and Lydia Rainey, "Central Office Leadership in Principal Professional Learning Communities: The Practice Beneath the Policy," *Teachers College Record* 116, no. 4 (2014); Meredith I. Honig, Nitya Venkateswaran, and Patricia McNeil, "Research Use as Learning: The Case of Fundamental Change in School District Central Offices," *American Educational Research Journal* 54, no. 5 (2017): 938–71.

About the Authors

Meredith I. Honig is a professor of Education Policy, Organizations, and Leadership at the University of Washington (UW), Seattle. Her research, teaching, and district partnerships focus on the interruption and rebuilding of inequitable school district practices and systems to ensure high-quality teaching and learning for each student, especially those historically underserved by public schools. Her work recognizes that barriers to educational equity are systemic, that school district central office leaders are in strategic positions to lead for systemic changes important to such results, and that they would benefit from new knowledge and support for their leadership.

Dr. Honig has examined and supported district leadership of various reform strategies, including: school-community partnerships, new small autonomous schools initiatives, data-informed decision-making, and districtwide teaching and learning improvement efforts. Her findings have been published in such journals as *Educational Researcher*, the *American Educational Research Journal*, and *Educational Evaluation and Policy Analysis* and funded by the Wallace Foundation, the Spencer Foundation, the W.T. Grant Foundation, and other sources.

In 2014, Dr. Honig and Lydia R. Rainey established the District Leadership Design Lab (DL2) to enable district leaders to access knowledge and tools to help them lead their own efforts to fundamentally transform their central offices into school support systems.

Between 2012 and 2018, Dr. Honig directed the Leadership for Learning (EdD) program, which won the 2016 Exemplary Educational Leadership Program award from the University Council for Educational Administration.

Prior to joining the UW-Seattle faculty, Dr. Honig was an assistant professor and codirector of the Center for Educational Policy and Leadership at the University of Maryland, College Park. She has worked at the California Department of Education and in other state and local youth-serving agencies. She received her AB from Brown University in Educational Studies and Public Policy and American Institutions and her PhD in Educational Administration and Policy Analysis from Stanford University.

Lydia R. Rainey is a research scientist at the UW-Seattle and the director of research for DL2. Since 2000, Dr. Rainey has researched ways to design and implement equitable school systems. Her recent research has focused on how education leaders in both central offices and schools implement policies that call for deep changes in their day-to-day work and how they use various forms of data and evidence in their decision-making. She approaches this work using traditional qualitative and quantitative techniques, as well as design-based research partnerships.

Prior to joining DL2, she worked with the UW-Bothell's Center on Reinventing Public Education, the UW-Seattle's Center for Teaching and Policy, and the City of Seattle Office of Education. Dr. Rainey has a PhD in Education Policy, Organizations, and Leadership, a master's of Public Administration from the Evans School of Public Affairs, and a BA in Political Economy, all from the UW-Seattle.

Index